THE REPORT OF
THE PRESIDENT'S NATIONAL

MAY 2 '88

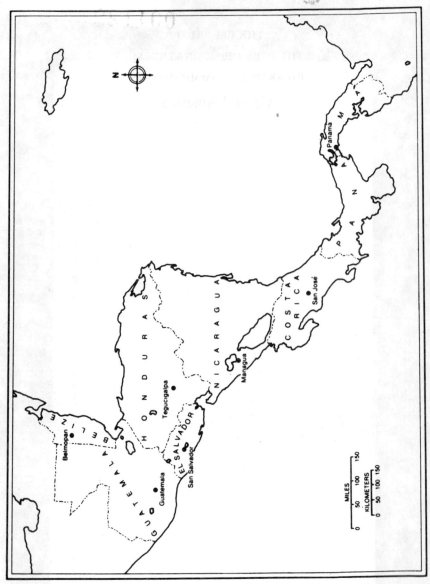

THE REPORT OF
THE PRESIDENT'S NATIONAL
BIPARTISAN COMMISSION ON
Central America

MACMILLAN PUBLISHING COMPANY

New York

Macmillan Publishing Company
866 Third Avenue, New York, N.Y. 10022
Collier Macmillan Canada, Inc.

ISBN 0-02-074610-5 (English-language edition)
0-02-074620-2 (Spanish-language edition)

Macmillan books are available at special discounts
for bulk purchases for sales promotions, premiums, fund-raising,
or educational use. Special editions or book excerpts
can also be created to specification.
For details, contact:
Special Sales Director
Macmillan Publishing Company
866 Third Avenue
New York, New York 10022

10 9 8 7 6 5 4 3 2 1

Designed by Jack Meserole

Printed in the United States of America

CHAIRMAN
DR. HENRY A. KISSINGER

COMMISSION MEMBERS:
MR. NICHOLAS F. BRADY
MAYOR HENRY G. CISNEROS
GOV. WILLIAM P. CLEMENTS, JR.
DR. CARLOS F. DIAZ-ALEJANDRO
MR. WILSON S. JOHNSON
MR. LANE KIRKLAND
MR. RICHARD M. SCAMMON
DR. JOHN SILBER
JUSTICE POTTER STEWART
AMB. ROBERT S. STRAUSS
DR. WILLIAM B. WALSH

EXECUTIVE DIRECTOR
AMB. HARRY W. SHLAUDEMAN

SENIOR COUNSELLORS:
REP. MICHAEL D. BARNES
SEN. LLOYD BENTSEN
REP. WILLIAM S. BROOMFIELD
SEN. PETE V. DOMENICI
SEN. DANIEL K. INOUYE
REP. JACK F. KEMP
AMB. JEANE KIRKPATRICK
MR. WINSTON LORD
SEN. CHARLES McC. MATHIAS
MR. WILLIAM D. ROGERS
REP. JAMES C. WRIGHT

THE NATIONAL BIPARTISAN COMMISSION
ON CENTRAL AMERICA

This is probably the first occasion on which the report of a Presidential Commission has been issued in both Spanish and English simultaneously, which should make it available to a much wider audience throughout the Spanish-speaking world, including readers of Spanish in the United States.

The Spanish edition of the Report of the National Bipartisan Commission on Central America is an expression of our deep respect for the people of the countries we visited. We are especially grateful to all the individuals, public officials and private citizens, who met with us and whose presentations contributed substantially to our report.

It is our hope that the Report will define an agenda for cooperation between the United States, the nations of Central America, the Contadora countries and all of Latin America.

Henry A. Kissinger

2201 C STREET NW., ROOM 1004, WASHINGTON, D.C. 20520.   TEL: (202) 632-7804

Executive Order 12433 of July 19, 1983

NATIONAL BIPARTISAN COMMISSION ON CENTRAL AMERICA

By the authority vested in me as President by the Constitution and laws of the United States of America, and in order to establish, in accordance with the provisions of the Federal Advisory Committee Act, as amended (5 U.S.C. App. I), the National Bipartisan Commission on Central America, it is hereby ordered as follows:

Section 1. *Establishment.* (a) There is established the National Bipartisan Commission on Central America. The Commission shall be composed of not more than 12 members appointed or designated by the President. These members shall be drawn from among distinguished leaders of the government, business, labor, education, Hispanic and religious communities. No more than seven members shall be of the same political party.

(b) The President shall designate a Chairman from among the members of the Commission.

Sec. 2. *Functions.* (a) The Commission shall study the nature of United States interests in the Central American region and the threats now posed to those interests. Based on its findings, the Commission shall provide advice to the President, the Secretary of State and the Congress on elements of a long-term United States policy that will best respond to the challenges of social, economic, and democratic development in the region, and to internal and external threats to its security and stability. The Commission also shall provide advice on means of building a national consensus on a comprehensive United States policy for the region.

(b) The Commission shall report to the President by December 1, 1983.

Sec. 3. *Administration.* (a) The heads of Executive agencies shall, to the extent permitted by law, provide the Commission such information as it may require for purposes of carrying out its functions.

(b) Members of the Commission shall serve without compensation for their work on the Commission. However, members appointed from among private citizens of the United States may, subject to the availability of funds, be allowed travel expenses, including per diem in lieu of subsistence, as authorized by law for persons serving intermittently in the government service (5 U.S.C. 5701–5707).

(c) The Secretary of State shall, to the extent permitted by law, provide the Commission with such administrative services, funds, facilities, staff and other support services as may be necessary for the performance of its functions.

Sec. 4. *General.* (a) Notwithstanding any other Executive Order, the functions of the President under the Federal Advisory Committee Act, as amended, which are applicable to the Commission, shall be performed by the Secretary of State, in accordance with guidelines and procedures established by the Administrator of General Services.

(b) The Commission shall, unless otherwise extended, terminate 60 days after submitting its final report.

THE WHITE HOUSE
July 19, 1983

By the authority vested in me as President by the Constitution and laws of the United States of America, including the Federal Advisory Committee Act, as amended (5 U.S.C. App. I), it is hereby ordered that Section 2 (b) of Executive Order No. 12433, establishing the National Bipartisan Commission on Central America, is amended to provide as follows:

"(b) The Commission shall report to the President by February 1, 1984.".

THE WHITE HOUSE
November 18, 1983

MEMBERS OF THE NATIONAL BIPARTISAN COMMISSION ON CENTRAL AMERICA

Ambassador Robert S. Strauss
Attorney at Law
Washington, D.C.

Dr. William B. Walsh
President, Project Hope
Bethesda, Maryland

SENIOR COUNSELLORS
TO THE COMMISSION

Ambassador Jeane Kirkpatrick
U.S. Permanent Representative to the United Nations
Washington, D.C.

Mr. Winston Lord
President, Council on Foreign Relations
New York, New York

Mr. William D. Rogers
Attorney at Law
Washington, D.C.

Senator Daniel K. Inouye (D., Hawaii)
Washington, D.C.

Senator Pete V. Domenici (R., New Mexico)
Washington, D.C.

Senator Lloyd Bentsen (D., Texas)
Washington, D.C.

Senator Charles McC. Mathias (R., Maryland)
Washington, D.C.

Representative William S. Broomfield (R., Michigan)
Washington, D.C.

Representative Jack F. Kemp (R., New York)
Washington, D.C.

Representative James C. Wright (D., Texas)
Washington, D.C.

Representative Michael D. Barnes (D., Maryland)
Washington, D.C.

The President
The White House
Washington, D.C.

Dear Mr. President:

In establishing the National Bipartisan Commission on Central America, you asked its advice on what would be appropriate elements of "a long-term United States policy that will best respond to the challenges of social, economic, and democratic development in the region, and to internal and external threats to its security and stability."

The analyses and recommendations in this report seek to respond to that request. However, as we studied the region and its problems—its crises—we found that the long-term challenge also requires short-term actions. In many respects the crisis is so acute, and the time-frame for response so limited, that immediate responses are a necessary element of any long-term policy. Thus to some extent we have discussed both, though we have tried to place such short-term recommendations as we make within the framework of a longer-term approach.

You also asked our advice on "means of building a national consensus on a comprehensive United States policy for the region." Our best advice on this is, I believe, embodied less in the specific language of the report than in its total message, which reflects the extraordinary experience of this Commission. Twelve members, of both political parties and of widely disparate views, studying the situation in Central America with intensity and dedication over a period of nearly six months, reached a degree of consensus at the end that I think few of us expected at the beginning. The lesson of this experience, I believe, is that the best route to consensus on U.S. policy toward Central America is by exposure to the realities of Central America.

On behalf of the members of the Commission, I wish to thank you for the opportunity you gave us to share this experience. We on the Commission hope that this report will contribute to a wider recognition of the urgency of the crisis in Central America, and to a deeper understanding both of its dimensions and of the opportunity it provides for a united people to help our neighbors toward a better future.

Respectfully,

Henry A. Kissinger
Chairman

The Commission	*Senior Counsellors*
Nicholas F. Brady	Jeane Kirkpatrick
Henry G. Cisneros	Winston Lord
William P. Clements, Jr.	William D. Rogers
Carlos F. Diaz-Alejandro	Daniel K. Inouye
Wilson S. Johnson	Pete V. Domenici
Lane Kirkland	Lloyd Bentsen
Richard M. Scammon	Charles McC. Mathias
John Silber	William S. Broomfield
Potter Stewart	Jack F. Kemp
Robert S. Strauss	James C. Wright
William B. Walsh	Michael D. Barnes

Harry W. Shlaudeman
   Executive Director

With great respect, we dedicate this report
to the late Senator Henry M. Jackson,
who proposed the creation of a bipartisan
commission on Central America and served as
one of its Senior Counsellors. In his life
and work Senator Jackson was devoted to the
twin goals of national security and human
betterment. These are also the goals that
have guided this report, and we hope, in his
spirit, that it will contribute to their
advancement.

CONTENTS

THE REPORT OF
THE PRESIDENT'S NATIONAL
BIPARTISAN COMMISSION ON
Central America

CHAPTER I

INTRODUCTION

FOR the members of this Commission, these past several months have been an extraordinary learning experience which we feel uniquely privileged to have shared.

In this report, we present an extensive set of concrete policy recommendations. But we also seek to share what we have learned with the people of the United States, and, based on what we have found, to suggest ways of thinking about Central America and its needs that may contribute to a more informed understanding in the future.

We hope, at the same time, to communicate something else we developed as a result of this experience: a sense of urgency about Central America's crisis, of compassion for its people, but also—cautiously—of hope for its future.

For most people in the United States, Central America has long been what the entire New World was to Europeans of five centuries ago: *terra incognita*. Probably few of even the most educated could name all the countries of Central America and their capitals, much less recite much of their political and social backgrounds.

Most members of this Commission began with what we now see as an extremely limited understanding of the region, its needs and its importance. The more we learned, the more convinced we became that the crisis there is real, and acute; that the United States must act to meet it, and act boldly; that the stakes are large, for the United States, for the hemisphere, and, most poignantly, for the people of Central America.

In this report, we propose significant attention and help to a previously neglected area of the hemisphere. Some, who have not studied the area as we have, may think this disproportionate, dismissing it as the natural reaction of a commission created to deal with a single subject. We think any such judgment would be a grave mistake.

It is true that other parts of the world are troubled. Some of these, such as the Middle East, are genuinely in crisis. But the crisis in Central America makes a particularly urgent claim on the United States for several reasons.

First, Central America is our near neighbor. Because of this, it critically involves our own security interests. But more than that, what happens on our doorstep calls to our conscience. History, contiguity, consanguinity—all these tie us to the rest of the Western Hemisphere; they also tie us very particularly to the nations of Central America. When Franklin Roosevelt proclaimed what he called his "Good Neighbor Policy," that was more than a phrase. It was a concept that goes to the heart of civilized relationships not only among people but also among nations. When our neighbors are in trouble, we cannot close our eyes and still be true to ourselves.

Second, the crisis calls out to us because we *can* make a difference. Because the nations are small, because they are near, efforts that would be minor by the standards of other crises can have a large impact on this one.

Third, whatever the short-term costs of acting now, they are far less than the long-term costs of not acting now.

Fourth, a great power can choose what challenges to respond to, but it cannot choose where those challenges come—or when. Nor can it avoid the necessity of deliberate choice. Once challenged, a decision not to respond is fully as consequential as a decision to respond. We are challenged now in Central America. No agony of indecision will make that challenge go away. No wishing it were easier will make it easier.

Perhaps the United States should have paid more attention to Central America sooner. Perhaps, over the years, we should have intervened less, or intervened more, or intervened differently. But all these are questions of what might have been. What confronts us now is a question of what might become. Whatever its roots in the past, the crisis in Central America exists urgently in the present, and its successful resolution is vital to the future.

How We Learned

Before discussing *what* we learned, we believe it would be helpful to indicate something of *how* we learned.

The Commission held 30 full days of regular meetings in Washington, plus another 12 special meetings. In all, we met in the United States with nearly 200 people who had something particular to contribute to our deliberations. These included President Reagan, Secretary of State Shultz, all three living former Presidents, four former Secretaries of State, members of Congress, the Joint Chiefs of Staff, and an exceptionally wide range of organizational representatives and private individuals with knowledge of the region and of the kinds of problems encountered in the region.

During nine days of foreign travel—six days in Central America, and three in Mexico and Venezuela—we heard from more than 300 officials and other witnesses and briefers. On its trips abroad, the Commission met not only with heads of government, cabinet members and legislative leaders, but also with leaders of the political opposition, journalists, educators, business and labor leaders, military experts, church officials, Indian leaders, representatives of private organizations, experts on health and social services, economists, agronomists—anyone who could broaden our outlook or deepen our understanding, including ordinary citizens from many walks of life. Similarly in this country, we sought the views of a wide variety of people and organizations, representing a wide variety of backgrounds and disciplines.

We sent detailed questionnaires to 170 selected outside experts. More than 230 other individuals and groups provided written materials, many of them extensive, for the Commission's use. All members of the Commission participated in the selection of those solicited for their views.

The entire operation amounted to an intensive seminar on Central America, conducted by what was probably the largest and most distinguished "faculty" on Central American issues ever assembled. Although we certainly did not become experts on the region in the same sense in which many of those we consulted are experts, we believe that we did become unusually well-informed laymen. And, in the process, we found that many of our perceptions changed.

What we have tried to bring to this report is essentially that well-informed layman's perspective, as influenced by the particular combinations of experience and values that, as individuals, we brought to the Commission. We have sought to apply that experience and those values to what we found in Central America, and to what we learned about Central America and the relationship between the crisis there and the larger world.

What We Learned

In the chapters that follow, we present our findings and recommendations in detail.

Chapter 2 places the Central American crisis within its larger hemispheric context, with particular emphasis on the twin challenges of rescuing the hemisphere's troubled economies and establishing principles of political legitimacy.

Chapter 3 places the crisis in historical perspective, tracing the background of the nations of Central America and the ways in which the crisis developed.

Chapter 4 examines the economic crisis in the region, and presents specific recommendations for measures that can be taken to meet it—both emergency short-term measures and others for the medium and longer term, together with a means of ensuring that economic, political and social development go forward together.

Chapter 5 focuses on what we call "human development" needs—particularly in health and education—and on what must and can be done to meet them.

Chapter 6 explores the security dimensions of the crisis, including Soviet and Cuban involvement, the problems of guerrilla war, the situation as it is today, what can be done to meet it, and what we recommend that the United States do to help.

Chapter 7 examines the diplomatic aspects, including routes which could be followed in seeking a negotiated solution.

Certain common threads run through all the chapters.

• First, the tortured history of Central America is such that neither the military nor the political nor the economic nor the social aspects of the crisis can be considered independently of the others. Unless rapid progress can be made on the political, economic and social fronts, peace on the military front will be elusive and would be fragile. But unless the externally supported insurgencies are checked and the violence curbed, progress on those other fronts will be elusive and would be fragile.

• Second, the roots of the crisis are both indigenous and foreign. Discontents are real, and for much of the population conditions of life are miserable; just as Nicaragua was ripe for revolution, so the conditions that invite revolution are present elsewhere in the region as well. But these conditions have been exploited by hostile outside forces—specifically, by Cuba, backed by the Soviet Union and now operating through Nicaragua—which will turn any revolution they capture into a totalitarian state, threatening the region and robbing the people of their hopes for liberty.

• Third, indigenous reform, even indigenous revolution, is not a security threat to the United States. But the intrusion of aggressive outside powers exploiting local grievances to expand their own political influence and military control is a serious threat to the United States, and to the entire hemisphere.

• Fourth, we have a humanitarian interest in alleviating misery and helping the people of Central America meet their social and economic needs, and together with the other nations of the hemisphere we have a national interest in strengthening democratic institutions wherever in the hemisphere they are weak.

• Fifth, Central America needs help, both material and moral, governmental and nongovernmental. Both the commands of conscience and calculations of our own national interest require that we give that help.

• Sixth, ultimately, a solution of Central America's problems will depend on the Central Americans themselves. They need our help, but our help alone will not be enough. Internal reforms, outside assistance, bootstrap efforts, changed economic policies —all are necessary, and all must be coordinated. And other nations with the capacity to do so not only in this hemisphere, but in Europe and Asia, should join in the effort.

• Seventh, the crisis will not wait. There is no time to lose.

No Room for Partisanship

If there is no time to lose, neither is the crisis in Central America a matter which the country can afford to approach on a partisan basis.

The people of Central America are neither Republicans nor Democrats. The crisis is nonpartisan, and it calls for a nonpartisan response. As a practical political matter, the best way to a nonpartisan policy is by a bipartisan route.

This Commission is made up of Republicans and Democrats, nonpolitical private citizens and persons active in partisan politics. It has members from business and labor, the academic world, the world of private organizations, former members of the executive, legislative and judicial branches of government; a former Senator and a former Governor, both Republicans; a Democratic Mayor and a former Democratic National Chairman; among the Senior Counsellors joining its deliberations have been members of both Houses of Congress from both parties. We are immensely grateful for the contribution made by those who served as Senior Counsellors, though we wish to point out that the conclusions we have drawn are those of the Commission itself and do not necessarily reflect the views of the Senior Counsellors.

We have approached our deliberations in a nonpartisan spirit and in a bipartisan way, and we believe that the nation can and must do the same.

Because the Commission has twelve members, each with strong individual views, there obviously are many things in this report to which individual members would have assigned different weight, or which they would have interpreted somewhat differently or put differently. Such is the nature of commissions. But these differences were personal, not partisan. This report, on balance, does represent what all of us found to be a quite remarkable consensus, considering the often polarized and emotional nature of the debate that has surrounded Central America. Among ourselves, we found a much greater degree of consensus at the end of our odyssey than at the beginning. This in itself gives us hope that the nation, too, as it learns more about Central America, its crisis and its needs, will find its way to a united determination to take and support the kind of measures that we believe are needed in the interests of the United States and of the hemisphere, and for the sake of the sorely beleaguered people of Central America.

CHAPTER 2

A HEMISPHERE IN TRANSFORMATION

THE COMMISSION has been asked to make recommendations on Central America. We recognize that our mandate has this geographic limit. But as we examined the isthmus it became apparent that the crisis which gave rise to this Commission is a part of a broader reality and that United States policy in Central America must reflect a clear understanding of its hemispheric framework.

The hemisphere as a whole is in flux. Central America's difficulties are enmeshed in the Latin American experience, which is different from our own.

Central America's present suffering is to an important degree the product of internal conditions which can also be found in Mexico and South America. Much of Latin America has an Indian heritage; most of it was colonized by Spain. In Central America, the mark of that experience has remained on attitudes, political processes and ways of doing things, as it has throughout the hemisphere to this day. The conflicts in the isthmus derive in part from social and economic structures whose origins, as in South America and Mexico, lie in the sixteenth, seventeenth and eighteenth centuries.

The crisis in Central America is also partially the result of events and forces outside the region. The soaring costs of imported energy, the drop in world coffee, sugar and other commodity prices, recession in the developed world, the explosion of international interest rates, have undermined economic progress. International terrorism, imported revolutionary ideologies, the ambitions of the Soviet Union, and the example and engagement of a Marxist Cuba are threatening the hopes for political progress.

Throughout history, the U.S. policies toward the nations of the Americas that have succeeded have been those that related the individuality and variety of the different countries to a concept of the hemisphere as a whole. The Monroe Doctrine, the Good Neighbor Policy of Franklin Roosevelt and the Alliance for Progress shared a recognition that despite the enormous differences among nations as ethnically, culturally, politically and historically diverse as, for example, Mexico, Guatemala, Costa Rica, Argentina, Peru and Brazil, there was a commonality of interest and experience calling not for uniformity but for coherence in our policies toward the many individual nations of Latin America. So it is today. The response of the United States to the conflict in Central America must take appropriate account of these national differences, but at the same time must relate our interests to those of the entire hemisphere in a way that evokes a sense of common purpose. Although it is beyond the scope of this Commission to recommend policies for the entire hemisphere, we have framed our recommendations with this broader context in mind.

The international purposes of the United States in the late twentieth century are cooperation, not hegemony or domination; partnership, not confrontation; a decent life for all, not exploitation. Those objectives must be achievable in this hemisphere if they can be realized anywhere.

Despite our different origins, the United States shares much with Latin America. We not only share a hemisphere, we share a history as well. Columbus's voyage, five centuries ago, helped shatter the old order of Europe, and opened the way to a truly New World.

We also share cultures, ideas and values. The colonial era and the overlapping of cultures have left in the U.S. South and West a permanent legacy of Spanish and Mexican architecture, customs, religion, law, patterns of land ownership, and place names. The idea of popular revolution to vindicate the right of people to govern themselves swept this part of the world first—nearly simultaneously in its English and Latin regions—a century and a half before the colonial empires of Africa and Asia began to

[9]

disappear. Although North and South America followed different paths of national development, the nations of the Western Hemisphere have been moved from the beginning of their histories by a common devotion to freedom from foreign domination, sovereign equality, and the right of people to determine the forms and methods of their own governance.

We also share economic interests. Of all U.S. private investment in the developing world, 62 percent is in Latin America and the Caribbean. Latin America is a major trading partner of this country, accounting for more than 15 percent of our exports and about the same share of our imports. Our consumers and our industries depend on the region for coffee, iron, petroleum and a host of other goods. The Panama Canal is a vital artery of our international commerce. The economies of Argentina, Brazil, Mexico and Venezuela are among the most advanced and diversified in the developing world, and also among the most heavily burdened with debt. They are major contributors to world trade; the way that together we deal with their debt problems will be decisive for the future of the international financial system.

We also share a community with Latin America. So many of our own citizens are of Latin origin that there is a special kinship in this hemisphere. The transcontinental sweep of the southern United States that stretches from Miami to Los Angeles, and which is home to many of our fastest growing urban areas and high technology industries, regards as a natural element of life its shared Gulf and Caribbean sea routes as well as a 2,000-mile land border facing south. Common time zones and short distances facilitate flows of information and constant travel for business, education, pleasure and employment.

The similarities should not be romanticized. Our historic experiences have not been the same. North America did not begin with an essentially feudal social structure, nor was military conquest as central to us as it was in Latin America's early history. The Iberian cultures planted different modes of thought, different attitudes. But despite these differences the Americas, North and South, have tried recurringly to shape a common destiny. The sense of interdependence and mutual reliance was manifest from the outset of the struggles for independence. It moved President Monroe to proclaim this hemisphere off limits to the territorial ambitions of European colonialism. That same sense of common destiny brought the Americas together in the first international organization for regional cooperation, the International Conference of American States in 1889–90. It led them some 60 years later to design—under the Treaty of Rio de Janeiro—the first mutual security system recognized by the U.N. Charter and to organize history's boldest venture of region-wide development in the Alliance for Progress in 1961.

We are aware that widespread ignorance about the area in this country is an obstacle, indeed a danger. We are also aware that our interests, our aspirations, and our capacity to grasp the essence of the complex reality of our age will be put to one of their most important tests in this hemisphere. This is the spirit with which we have approached our assignment of dealing with the prospects of a small but integral part of this hemisphere: Central America.

TWO CHALLENGES

The hemisphere is challenged both economically and politically. While that double challenge is common to all of Latin America, it now takes its most acute form in Central America.

The Economic Challenge

First, the commanding economic issue in all of Latin America is the impoverishment of its people. The nations of the hemisphere—not least those of Central America—advanced remarkably throughout the 1960's and 1970's. Growth was strong, though not nearly enough was done to close the gap between the rich and the poor, the product of longstanding economic, social and political structures.

But then the situation turned down. Imported energy costs went up in the 1970's, while commodities prices fell. The developed countries went into recession. Many Latin American governments responded by borrowing in the hope that an early revival would allow them to carry their newly expanded indebtedness. Instead, the cost of servicing that debt began to rise rapidly, as international interest rates—spurred by anti-inflationary monetary policy in the U.S.—shot upwards. The nations of Latin America—including key countries in Central America—were forced to alter course sharply, cutting public expenditures on schools, health services, and roads, restraining growth and personal incomes, slashing imports and raising taxes along with exchange rates. The consequence has been that standards of living, already low in comparison to the developed world and badly skewed, have been cut back across the board.

What appears to the international financial system as a debt crisis has a profound human dimension in the area of this Commission's primary concern, as it does throughout Latin America. Joblessness is up. Malnutrition and infant mortality have escalated. Poverty was pernicious in Latin America even during the growth years. Fifteen years ago, at the Conference in Medellin, Colombia, the Catholic Church spoke of the need for a "preferential option" to concentrate public policy and public effort on a social ethic of responsibility for the poor. That need is more pressing today. Poverty is on the rise everywhere in Latin America.

No Central American policy for the United States worth its name can fail to meet this economic, social and financial challenge, nor can we deal with Central America in isolation from the rest of the hemisphere. The contraction of the hemisphere's economies, and the impoverishment of its people, must be reversed. Real growth must be restored.

The Political Challenge

Second, the political challenge in the hemisphere centers on the legitimacy of government. Once again, this takes a particularly acute form in Central America.

Powerful forces are on the march in nearly every country of the hemisphere, testing how nations shall be organized and by what processes authority shall be established and legitimized. Who shall govern and under what forms are the central issues in the process of change now under way in country after country throughout Latin America and the Caribbean.

Brazil is in mid-political passage, from almost two decades of military rule to popular elections of a civilian chief executive, an independent legislature, civilian ministries and a multi-party political system.

Argentina has elected its first civilian president in years, restoring democracy and civilian control of government. Ecuador ended military rule and elected its own civilian president in 1979; Peru did the same in 1980. In the Dominican Republic, free and uncorrupted elections have become the rule. Venezuela's own democracy remains vigorous, as was evident in its elections of December 1983, in which 92 percent of the eligible voters participated. Colombia's democracy is equally strong. In fact, only a handful of nations in Latin America today are ruled through political systems closed to the prospects of elections.

In short, democracy is becoming the rule rather than the exception. The nations of Central America are also, each in its own fashion, engaged in a struggle over how a nation shall be governed. Panama expects to elect a civilian president next year in an open and fair process. Costa Rica made its choice years ago and is living under an authentic democratic system—and it is no accident that Costa Rica is the least violent society, the nation of the region most free of repression and the one whose relations with the United States are most particularly warm. Honduras has held a free election, choosing a civilian president with a strong reputation for impressive leadership. Guatemala is attempting to arrange an election for a Constituent Assembly this year. El Salvador is in transition; its present provisional administration is the result of a demonstration of popular will in 1982. In March 1984 it will elect a president under a permanent constitution. Of the nations in the region, only the Sandinista leadership in Nicaragua, perhaps intending to imitate the political arrangements in Cuba, has been ambiguous about—if not hostile to—what would be accepted by the international community as open, multi-party political contests. But even the Sandinistas face strong demands from both inside and outside the nation, especially from nearby democratic countries such as Venezuela and Costa Rica, that they return to the ideals of the democratic revolution against Somoza and keep their promise of free elections made in 1979 to the Organization of American States.

[13]

Experience has destroyed the argument of the old dictators that a strong hand is essential to avoid anarchy and communism, and that order and progress can be achieved only through authoritarianism. Those nations in Latin America which have been moving to open their political, social and economic structures and which have employed honest and open elections have been marked by a stability astonishing in the light of the misery which still afflicts the hemisphere. The modern experience of Latin America suggests that order is more often threatened when people have no voice in their own destinies. Social peace is more likely in societies where political justice is founded on self-determination and protected by formal guarantees.

The issue is not what particular system a nation might choose when it votes. The issue is rather that nations should choose for themselves, free of outside pressure, force or threat. There is room in the hemisphere for differing forms of governance and different political economies. Authentically indigenous changes, and even indigenous revolutions, are not incompatible with international harmony in the Americas. They are not incompatible even with the mutual security of the members of the inter-American system—if they are truly indigenous. The United States can have no quarrel with democratic decisions, as long as they are not the result of foreign pressure and external machinations. The Soviet-Cuban thrust to make Central America part of their geostrategic challenge is what has turned the struggle in Central America into a security and political problem for the United States and for the hemisphere.

There is no self-determination when there is foreign compulsion or when nations make themselves tools of a strategy designed in other continents.

THREE PRINCIPLES

For most of the first 200 years of its history, the United States turned its eyes primarily towards Europe. Tradition, trans-Atlantic alliances, cultural ties, even the physical location of the Eastern centers of power focused attention in this country on relations with such nations as Britain, France, Italy and Germany. For the United States, the Atlantic Alliance has been the central strategic relationship.

In the years since World War II, as Asia emerged as a center of both political conflict and economic power, the United States began to look westward—fighting two Asian wars, forging Asian ties, strengthening its role as a Pacific power. Through all this time, whether looking east or west, the United States focused its attention only intermittently on the South.

As a result, the ties that bind this nation to Latin America have rarely been expressed in American foreign policy as firmly and consistently as the reality of our interdependence demands. We have tended to view the region superficially, too often stereotypically; our policy has sometimes swung erratically between the obsessive and the negligent. The 1980's must be the decade in which the United States recognizes that its relationships with Mexico and Central and South America rank in importance with its ties to Europe and Asia.

And we require a design to express that interest. The Monroe Doctrine has sometimes been challenged by our neighbors to the south—especially in some of its unilateral interpretations. But they have never questioned its central inspiration: the vision of a hemisphere united by a core of common commitment to independence and liberty, insulated from other quarrels, free to work out its own destiny in its own way, yet ready to play as constructive a role in world affairs as its resources might permit.

In any event, the challenges of today are not the challenges of 1823. A contemporary doctrine of U.S.-Latin American relations cannot rest on insulating the hemisphere from foreign influence. It must also respond in an affirmative way to the economic and political challenges in the hemisphere; U.S. policy must respect the diversities among the nations of America even while advancing their common interests. Three principles should, in the Commission's view, guide hemispheric relations; we have sought to apply them to our considerations of Central America.

The first principle is democratic self-determination.

The vitality of the Inter-American system lies now more than ever before in accepting a firm commitment of its member nations to political pluralism, freedom of expression, respect for human rights, the maintenance of an independent and effective system of justice and the right of people to choose their destiny in free elections without repression, coercion or foreign manipulation. The essence of our effort together must be the legitimation of governments by free consent—the rejection of violence and murder as political instruments, of the imposition of authority from above, the use of the power of the state to suppress opposition and dissent. Instead we must do all we can to nurture democracy in this hemisphere.

The second principle is encouragement of economic and social development that fairly benefits all.

The encroachments of poverty must be stopped, recession reversed, and prosperity advanced. Adherence to this principle involves something deeper than meeting a short-term emergency. It means laying the basis for sustained and broadbased economic growth. There must be encouragement of those incentives that liberate and energize a free economy. There must be an end to the callous proposition that some groups will be "have-nots" forever. Any set of policies for the hemisphere must address the need to expand the economies of its nations and revive the hopes of its people.

The third principle is cooperation in meeting threats to the security of the region.

The present international framework for dealing with challenges to the mutual security of the Americas is weak. With respect to Central America, the Inter-American system has failed to yield a coordinated response to the threat of subversion and the use of Soviet and Cuban proxies, which have become endemic since the day when the instruments of Inter-American cooperation were first drawn up.

A modernizing of the regional security system is imperative. Just as there can be no real security without economic growth and social justice, so there can be no prosperity without security. The Soviet and Cuban threat is real. No nation is immune from terrorism and the threat of armed revolution supported by Moscow and Havana with imported arms and imported ideology. The nations of Latin America—and of each of its regions, as is being demonstrated in Central America—have authentic local collective security interests. These should be expressed in new mechanisms for regional cooperation and consultation, and in a commitment to common action in defense of democracy adapted to the special circumstances and interests of the nations affected. Otherwise the temptations of unilateralism will become overwhelming.

In the past, other parts of the hemisphere have been the focal points of turbulence. Today's concentration of crises is in Central America. The chapters that follow focus on that region, and set forth the specific political, economic and security measures which the Commission believes are necessary. We see *no* way to avoid a comprehensive effort to respond to these issues together. The remainder of this report sets forth the ways in which this Commission believes a consistent economic, political and security effort, one which coordinates the best efforts of the people in Central America, its neighbors, and the United States, can be maintained. The way in which that combination of crises is addressed—or any failure to address it with both the urgency and the comprehensiveness it requires—will profoundly affect not only our national interest but the larger interests of the hemisphere as well.

CHAPTER 3

CRISIS IN CENTRAL AMERICA: AN HISTORICAL OVERVIEW

CENTRAL AMERICA is gripped today by a profound crisis. That crisis has roots deep in the region's history, but it also contains elements of very recent origin. An understanding of it requires some familiarity with both.

The impact of the crisis on the people of Central America has been shattering. Its potential impact on the hemisphere, on the United States, and, in a larger sense, on the world, is far-reaching.

If this crisis were a purely local matter, involving the peoples of that region alone, it would still deserve the urgent attention of the people of the United States as a matter of simple humanity. Its larger dimensions give us, in addition, strong reasons of national self-interest to be acutely concerned about its outcome.

There has been considerable controversy, sometimes vigorous, as to whether the basic causes of the crisis are indigenous or foreign. In fact, the crisis is the product of *both* indigenous and foreign factors. It has sources deep in the tortured history and life of the region, but it has also been powerfully shaped by external forces. Poverty, repression, inequity, all were there, breeding fear and hate; stirring in a world recession created a potent witch's brew, while outside forces have intervened to exacerbate the area's troubles and to exploit its anguish.

Those outside forces have given the crisis more than a Central American dimension. The United States is not threatened by indigenous change, even revolutionary change, in Central America. But the United States must be concerned by the intrusion into Central America of aggressive external powers.

In this chapter, we will explore the origins of the crisis and try to define its present nature. This requires a brief excursion into the region's history. That history is complex and in some respects controversial. We neither attempt nor pretend to present a comprehensive, definitive treatment of it. Rather, our aim is to give enough background to place the crisis in perspective, and to trace through certain trends that are important to any consideration of prospects and policies for the future.

This chapter deals principally with the five nations of the Organization of Central American States: El Salvador, Honduras, Nicaragua, Guatemala and Costa Rica. A sixth country, Belize, is geographically within Central America but its political, economic and cultural ties are primarily with the Caribbean. A seventh, Panama, is affected by the regional crisis but emerged in a different historical context. The term "Central America" tends to be rather loosely and variously defined—sometimes as the five, sometimes as the seven, sometimes rather vaguely to include other contiguous parts of North and South America. In this report, we will generally include the seven for purposes of economic and social programs, while focusing our discussion of the security and diplomatic crises on the five. With respect to the latter, we follow the usage employed by the so-called Contadora Group (Mexico, Venezuela, Panama and Colombia), which is assisting in the effort to resolve the conflicts within and among the five.

The Land

A bridge linking two continents, the Central American isthmus winds in a serpentine arc between the Pacific Ocean and Caribbean Sea, stretching 1500 miles from the base of the Yucatan Peninsula to the Colombian border. It is dominated by an imposing range of volcanic mountains, whose rugged patterns have presented obstacles to commerce, communications, and cultivation. The mountains are punctuated by breaks in Panama, Honduras, and Nicaragua that have tantalized travellers and entrepreneurs with visions of a trans-oceanic passage. The mountains, where at altitudes from 3,000 to 8,000 feet the bulk of the Central American population lives, provide a spring-like, salubrious climate that contrasts with the pestilential rain forest, bush jungles, and swampy marshlands of the two coasts.

Central America is located geographically in a high-risk area. Three tectonic plates meet along the isthmus, pushing against each other relentlessly and creating several major and hundreds of minor geological faults. Earthquakes, which occur with alarming frequency, have destroyed cities, disrupted commerce, created human misery, and even altered political history. Lava flows and pollution have similarly wreaked havoc on town and farm. The Caribbean coast is in the hurricane belt, where high winds and rains have regularly wiped out settlements and set back efforts at tropical cultivation. The coming of rainfall in a single season between June and November is frequently followed by long droughts, presenting monumental problems to agriculture, navigation, and road travel.

The Colonial Legacy

Both conquest and the colonial experience left marks on Central America that have greatly hindered political and economic development. Except in a few areas, the Spanish conquerors imposed on the Indian peoples a semi-feudal system based on large land holdings and the exploitation of indigenous labor. These patterns persisted from generation to generation into our day, with wealth, education, and political power continuing to be shared unequally between the descendents of the conquerors and those of the conquered.

The modern history of Central America traces back to a "Kingdom of Guatemala," which gradually emerged in the middle of the sixteenth century. It was a product of synthesis, growing out of a struggle between rival Spanish conquistadores from the vice royalties of Peru and "New Spain," as Mexico was then called. One *audiencia* (judiciary/legislature) was established in Panama under Peruvian auspices, and another was established in Guatemala, nominally subservient to Mexico, encompassing the present-day countries of Costa Rica, Nicaragua, Honduras, Guatemala, and El Salvador plus the Mexican state of Chiapas.

During the three centuries of Spanish colonial rule, roughly from the 1520's to the 1820's, Central America's political system was authoritarian; the economy was exploitative and mercantilist; the society was elitist, hierarchical and made up essentially of but two sharply distinct classes; and both the Church and the educational system reinforced the patterns of authoritarianism. Nor did the colonial period ever provide much training in self-governance; the large indigenous populations were never integrated into the political life of the colonies.

There were variations up and down the isthmus, however. Guatemala had the most gold and silver for the Spaniards to take and the most Indians to exploit. Hence the impact of the Spanish colonial system was strongest in that country, leaving a legacy of political and social structures particularly resistant to change. Panama and Costa Rica, with small indigenous populations, little gold or silver, and located far from the main centers of Spanish rule, felt the Spanish colonial impact the least. El Salvador, Honduras, and Nicaragua occupied intermediate positions.

Independence and After

Independence from Spain brought a fragmentation of political authority but otherwise little to alter the social institutions and practices of three centuries. The five nations began independent life in 1823 as one: the United Provinces of Central America. From the outset civil wars disrupted the effort to consolidate a central government. Just 15 years later the union dissolved and the five went their separate ways. The isthmus became a region of what some have called city-states: small countries weak and vulnerable to outside forces, and with reduced possibility for economic growth and diversification. Professor Ralph Lee Woodward's widely read history of the area bears the title *Central America, a Nation Divided*.

Political independence brought with it no accompanying social or economic revolution. The new Central American nations retained important characteristics established in the colonial era:

- Economies based on plantation agriculture.
- A concentration of large land holdings in a few hands (except for Costa Rica).

- Societies lacking vigorous middle classes and dominated by the landowning elites (again, except in Costa Rica).
- Poor communications within the region and relative isolation from the outside world.
- Habits of authoritarian government.
- Ingrained reliance on centralized state jurisdiction and tolerance of corruption.

Politically, the five nations called themselves republics and adopted constitutions modeled in many respects on the U.S. Constitution of 1787 and on the liberal Spanish constitution of 1812. The resulting governments had presidential and electoral systems resembling those of the United States. But the substance was very different. Judicial traditions based on the Roman civil law served primarily to facilitate state control rather than as a bulwark of individual rights. The difficulties that arose from trying to reconcile two systems, one political and the other legal, with distinctly different foundations are still apparent in Central America today.

The first 30 years of independent life were chaotic for the five republics. As elsewhere in Spanish America, political parties labeled as "Liberal" and "Conservative" battled over the role of the state and church-state relations. Local leaders—*caudillos*—at the head of armed bands contended for power. Disorder and violent conflict afflicted the region. Central America had repudiated its colonial institutions, yet it had not begun to develop free institutions to replace them.

From the 1850's to the 1880's, after the first generation of men-on-horseback had died off, some order was brought out of the chaos. The "Liberal" parties, with their strong commitment to commerce, came to power all across Central America, and for the most part they succeeded in establishing stable governments. But in this climate of greater order the landholding elites began to reconsolidate their power, while governments remained autocratic, generally under a single dictatorial leader.

Rule by Oligarchy

The period 1890–1930 was the heyday of oligarchic rule in Central America. In addition to the older landed oligarchy, a commercial import/export class had arisen. A coffee boom that began in Costa Rica in the 1870's transformed the export economies of Central America, providing substantial new wealth. Middle classes began to develop. Unwritten rules were established enabling the elites—whether military or civilian or, more usually, a combination of the two—to rotate or alternate in office. Military forces, which had largely been bands of irregulars in the service of powerful individuals, began to come under central authority and to develop into regular armies. This provided an important new avenue of upward mobility for ambitious young men, and transformed the politics of the region as the armies increasingly grew into autonomous institutions.

All these changes occurred under oligarchic auspices except in Costa Rica, which built upon its earlier democratic roots. Thus when the depression of the 1930's precipitated political and economic convulsions, Central America had no political infrastructure—parties, regular elections, representative institutions—out of which democracy could emerge.

By the first decades of the twentieth century, common characteristics in the economic development of the five republics had become apparent. The cultivation of a few basic agricultural crops for export—coffee, bananas and sugar—dominated their economies. Particularly after the coffee boom of the 1870's, plantations producing for export encroached on subsistence farming. A dual agricultural system emerged: large plantations for export crops; small plots to raise food. This reinforced the social divisions inherited from the colonial period. The bulk of the population survived on seasonal plantation labor at minimal wages, and on subsistence agriculture. A small group of families controlling the most productive land constituted the dominant elite. Export-oriented growth generated pockets of modernization and higher living standards in the urban areas. But the middle classes remained weak.

Stirrings of Change

The period of the 1930's was terribly disruptive in Central America. As the bottom dropped out of the market for Central America's products, a wave of instability swept the region; for the first time traditional oligarchic rule came under serious challenge. In El Salvador, Honduras, Guatemala, and Nicaragua new dictators appeared. While they typically ruled with strong-arm methods, they also often represented previously excluded middle classes. Having restored order, these dictators encouraged some economic development and social modernization, and they enjoyed a degree of popularity—at least for a time.

By this point, two main political traditions were operating in Central America—and an emerging third one.

First, there was the old authoritarian tradition. This historically dominant force still drew considerable strength from the difficulty of establishing democratic forms in the fragmented, violent, disintegrative context of Central America.

Second, there was a democratic tradition enshrined in political constitutions but of only marginal importance in practice. The democratic preference did emerge from time to time (in Guatemala in 1944, Honduras in 1957, El Salvador in 1972), but it lacked the practical roots democracy has had in the United States and elsewhere in the West. Except in Costa Rica, it was not institutionalized in the form of political parties and workable representative structures.

The third strain—socialism—also appeared in a variety of forms in Central America amid the turmoil of the 1930's and has remained present ever since, frequently mixed into both democratic (as in Costa Rica) and Marxist or even communist elements.

The problem for Central America was to devise a political formula capable of dealing with these diverse tendencies, none of which could command absolute majority support, and each of which was unacceptable to at least some of the main contenders for power in these societies.

Only in Costa Rica was the final formula democratic. After a brief but decisive civil war in 1948, regular elections have since led to periodic rotation in power by the two dominant groups.

Elsewhere, efforts were made to combine or reconcile the traditional and the liberal orientations, and at times even to hint at the socialist one.

In Nicaragua, for example, after the death of Anastasio Somoza García (1896–1956), his elder son Luis made various attempts to relax the harsher aspects of the old authoritarianism—to allow a greater sense of pluralism and freedom. In Honduras, military and civilian parties rotated in office or else ruled jointly in an arrangement whereby military officers controlled security matters and acted as political arbiters, while the civilian elites managed the economy, held key cabinet positions, and staffed the bureaucracy. In Guatemala, after the United States helped bring about the fall of the Arbenz government in 1954, politics became more divisive, violent and polarized than in the neighboring states. But even there, there were efforts to combine civilian and military rule, or to alternate between them, in various shaky and uneasy blends.

In El Salvador a similar system operated from 1958 to 1972. There, a group of younger, more nationalistic officers came to power and pursued populist strategies. They allowed the major trade union organizations to grow and to have a measure of political participation. The Army created its own political party, modeled after the Mexican PRI. It held elections regularly, in which the official candidates generally won; on the other hand, through a system of corporate representation within the party, most major groups had some say in national affairs.

None of these regimes was truly democratic, but the trend seemed to favor the growth of centrist political forces and to be leading toward greater pluralism and more representative political orders. This trend gave hope for peaceful accommodations and realistic responses to the profound social changes occurring in the countries of Central America.

Political Retrogression

The trend of the 1960's toward more open political systems was reversed during the 1970's. Whereas in Honduras the military sponsored moderate reform and prepared the country for a return to democracy, a period of closed political systems, repression and intransigence began in Guatemala, Nicaragua, and El Salvador. In each of these three countries, resistance to change on the part of the dominant military and civilian groups became stronger as demands for a larger share of national income, increased social services and greater political participation spread

[25]

from the middle class to the masses of the urban and rural poor. The armed forces tightened their control over the day-to-day activities of government and more harshly repressed perceived challenges to their power from trade union or political movements.

In Nicaragua, the political opening that had seemed to be promised in the 1960's was now closed off by Somoza's second son, Anastasio, Jr., who took power in 1966. His rule was characterized by greed and corruption so far beyond even the levels of the past that it might well be called a kleptocracy; it included a brazen reaping of immense private profits from international relief efforts following the devastating earthquake of 1972. And as opposition to his regime increased, repression became systematic and increasingly pervasive.

In Guatemala, the more or less centrist civilian and military governments of the 1960's gave way in the 1970's to a succession of extremely repressive regimes. The administrations of General Eugenio Laugerud and General Fernando Romero Lucas were among the most repressive either in the recent history of the hemisphere or in Guatemala's own often bloody past. Possibilities for accommodation, assimilation, and further democratization thus faded.

In El Salvador, the pattern was similar. Military-based regimes that had been moderately progressive in the early 1960's had become corrupt and repressive by the 1970's. The annulment of the victory by civilian Christian Democratic candidate José Napoleón Duarte in the 1972 election ushered in a period of severely repressive rule. It was in this context, with its striking parallels to the developments in Nicaragua and Guatemala, that the present crisis in El Salvador began.

It is no accident that these three countries—El Salvador, Guatemala, and Nicaragua—are precisely where the crisis for U.S. policy is centered. While there were of course significant national variations, all three went through a roughly parallel process in which a trend toward more open, pluralistic, and democratic societies gave way to oppression and polarization, precipitating the crisis which has now spread throughout Central America.

Modernization and Poverty: The Economic Background of the Crisis

The economic developments of the post-war period—modernization, rising expectations, persisting poverty, and ultimately the economic shock of the late 1970's—also helped set the stage for the present crisis.

The period between the coming of World War II and the early 1970's was one of sustained growth. War and the post-war boom in the developed world revived the international markets for Central America's commodity exports. By the middle of this century many Central Americans had come to realize that some form of common action by the five might help to overcome the obstacles to modernization and development created by history and small national size.

The idea of union had never quite died in Central America. It was therefore natural enough that the post-war experience in Europe and the maxims of the Economic Commission for Latin America (ECLA) under Raul Prebisch focused Central America's attention in the 1950's on the possibility of economic unity. On December 13, 1960, representatives of the five republics meeting in Managua signed the General Treaty for Central American Integration, leading to the establishment of the Central American Common Market.

The Common Market inspired a surge of energy and optimism throughout the region. Manufacturing for import substitution produced significant industrialization, particularly in Guatemala and El Salvador. Intra-regional trade grew from only $33 million in 1960 to over $1 billion in 1980, a proportional increase two and a half times greater than the growth in world trade during these decades. New regional institutions, such as the Central American Bank for Economic Integration and the Central American Economic Council, held out the promise of region-wide growth and development based on close cooperation among the five nations.

The Common Market, along with the external resources provided under the Alliance for Progress, made a substantial contribution to what the ECLA has described as a "sustained dynamism'' in the region's economy in the 1960's. Generally favorable and stable international prices for Central America's export commodities also contributed to this dynamic economic growth. The region's exports went up dramatically, rising from $250 million in 1950 to $3.2 billion in 1978. Gross domestic product in the region increased at a rate of 5.3 percent per year in real terms between 1950 and 1978. Incomes calculated on a per capita basis rose at rates all the more impressive because they were accompanied by population growth with few parallels in the world. The five republics had a population of less than eight million in 1950, and of more than 20 million by the end of the 1970's. Yet between those years real per capita income doubled.

Post-war growth brought a sharp increase in urbanizaton. Capital cities doubled their share of the total population. New highways and port facilities were built. Telephone and electric systems were expanded. More people got access to radio and television. Advances were made in health and education. Old centers of social power such as the armed forces and the Roman Catholic Church lost some of their homogeneity in the face of new ideological currents. Central American societies became more complex. New middle groups emerged, especially in the mushrooming cities, but the gulf between the rich and the mass of the very poor remained.

Although some benefitted from social change and economic growth in those decades, many others benefitted little or not at all. In ECLA's judgment—and the other experts the Commission consulted on this point were in virtually unanimous agreement—''the fruits of the long period of economic expansion were distributed in a flagrantly inequitable manner.'' Thus, as an example, in El Salvador in 1980, 66 percent of the national income went to the richest 20 percent of the population, 2 percent went to the poorest 20 percent. According to ECLA's data, over 60 percent of the region's population was living in poverty, over 40 percent in ''extreme poverty.'' The real incomes of poor families in Guatemala were actually lower in 1980 than in 1970.

While measures of absolute poverty are inevitably arbitrary and subject to considerable margins of error, studies show that in El Salvador, Guatemala, Honduras, and Nicaragua during the 1970's about half of the urban population and three-quarters of the rural population could not satisfy their basic needs in terms of nutrition, housing, health, and education. The population explosion magnified the problem of inequitable distribution of national income. As we have seen, the number of Central Americans almost tripled in 30 years. The World Bank projects a further increase in the region's population to 38 million by the end of the century. Except in Costa Rica, rapid urbanization and population growth overwhelmed the limited resources that governments were prepared to devote to social services—or that private organizations could provide. This was true in all fields—education, health, housing, and nutrition.

In short, the economic growth of the 60's and 70's did not resolve the region's underlying social problems. About 60 percent of the populations of El Salvador, Guatemala, Honduras, and Nicaragua (before the revolution) remained illiterate. Ten of every one hundred babies born died before the age of five, and, according to reliable nutritionists, 52 percent of the children were malnourished. Somewhere between four and five million people in the region were unemployed or underemployed. They and their families were often living on the edge of starvation.

The international economic crisis that developed in the late 1970's worsened the situation dramatically. World inflation, including the second steep jump in international petroleum prices in the decade, hit the five countries hard. (Only Guatemala among them has any domestic oil production of its own.) At the same time, the escalation in international interest rates drove up the annual cost of servicing external debt, a particularly stringent circumstance for democratic Costa Rica. Economic stagnation in the developed world also had a marked impact on Central American economies, which are especially vulnerable to the volatility of commodity prices. As a consequence of these factors, the region's exports now buy 30 percent less in imports than they did five years ago. By contrast, oil-importing developing countries as a group worldwide increased their export purchasing by more than 7 percent during this period.

The economic collapse of the late 1970's, coming as it did after a period of relatively sustained growth, shattered the rising hopes of Central Americans for a better life. Though the period of modernization by no means lifted most Central Americans out of poverty, it did arouse expectations that the quality of life would improve. The frustration of these expectations, along with the disappointment of efforts to bring about political change in the region, thus offered fertile opportunities for those both in the region and outside of it who wished to exploit the crisis for their own advantage.

The Growth of Communist Insurgency

By 1979, in terms of modern military capabilities Cuba had become perhaps the strongest power in the Western Hemisphere south of the United States. It was also the country best prepared and most eager to exploit the intensifying crisis in Central America.

During the preceding two decades, the Cuban revolution had already had a major effect in Central America. Castro's successful insurgency was studied eagerly in the universities, where the attraction of revolutionary Marxism was already strong. Castroism was initially seen as a dynamic deviation from the mainstream Soviet-sponsored communist movements, and it spawned would-be revolutionary groups in all the countries of the isthmus.

The influence of Castroism also produced schisms in the small Moscow-linked parties of the region. They mostly held to the orthodox view that, in the conditions then prevailing, armed insurgency was an unworkable strategy. But during the 1970's, as political and economic conditions worsened, that view came under increasing challenge. At the same time, conservatives and the military were frightened by the Cuban revolution into hardening their attitudes toward political change.

In the early years, the major Cuban effort to export revolution to Central America occurred in Guatemala. There, Castro gave support to an armed insurgency that began in 1960. Though the Soviet Union was relatively inactive after the Cuban Missile Crisis, Castro provided arms, financing and training to the MR-13 guerrilla movement and later to the rival Armed Forces of Revolution (FAR). This was not an isolated tactic. Cuba was following the same practice in this period with similar movements in Venezuela, Colombia and Peru. Indeed, it was the discovery of Cuban arms landed in Venezuela which resulted in the OAS decision to require the other members to cut trade and diplomatic ties.

The Guatemalan Army's successful counter-insurgency campaigns, Castro's increasing disappointment over the factional infighting of the Guatemalan guerrillas, and his disillusionment with the effort generally to export revolution to Latin America (climaxed by Che Guevara's defeat and death in Bolivia), greatly reduced the guerrilla threat in Guatemala by 1968.

In the succeeding years, and after Castro's decision to support the invasion of Czechoslovakia, the Cubans seemed to adopt the Soviet strategy of attempting to fashion normal diplomatic and commercial relations with a variety of governments in the hemisphere, while downplaying the revolutionary mission. Diplomatic ties were established with such leading countries as Argentina, Peru, Chile (before Allende's fall), Venezuela and Colombia. Contacts were opened with the United States and, in 1975, the U.S. cooperated in the OAS to eliminate the mandatory nature of that organization's sanctions against Cuba. Castro's venture into Angola put an end for a time to the U.S. effort to establish a basis for understanding with Cuba. But negotiations resumed two years later and led to the opening of diplomatic offices ("interest sections") in the two capitals. However, widening Cuban military involvement in Africa and Castro's unwillingness to discuss the question of Cuba's foreign interventions prevented further movement toward normalization of relations.

In 1978 Castro disappointed those who thought he had abandoned the export of revolution in this hemisphere. He saw new opportunities. Guerrillas were once again in the field in Guatemala; the elements of a promising insurgency were present in El Salvador; and, above all, a particularly inviting situation presented itself in Nicaragua where the Somoza dictatorship was beginning to crumble. The United States was still suffering the after-effects of Vietnam and Watergate. At the same time, Castro's Soviet patrons, who had not actively supported the armed struggle during the 1960's, were coming around to his view that the time for guerrilla war in Central America had arrived.

Their conversion to the doctrine of armed violence became complete with the collapse of Somoza in Nicaragua. Although Venezuela, Costa Rica, Panama, and other Latin American coun-

[31]

tries assisted the revolutionaries in Nicaragua, and although the refusal of the U.S. to supply arms helped precipitate Somoza's fall, Cuban support was a particularly important factor in the Sandinista triumph. It was Castro who unified the three Nicaraguan guerrilla factions and provided the weapons, supplies, and advisers that enabled the Cuban-oriented *comandantes* to establish themselves as the dominant group in the revolution.

Cuban and now also Nicaraguan support was subsequently critical in building the fighting forces of the Farabundo Martí Liberation Front in El Salvador, in maintaining them in the field, and in forcing them to unite in a combined effort in spite of the deep-seated distrust among the guerrilla factions. Indeed, it was a meeting hosted by Castro in December 1979 that had produced agreement among the Salvadoran insurgent factions to form a coordinating committee, as was publicly announced the following month.

In March 1982, the Chairman of the Intelligence Oversight Committee of the U.S. House of Representatives stated that there was "persuasive evidence that the Sandinista government of Nicaragua is helping train [Salvadoran] insurgents and is transferring arms and support from and through Nicaragua to the insurgents. They are further providing the insurgents with bases of operation in Nicaragua. Cuban involvement in providing arms— is also evident." Specifically, Nicaragua's position on the isthmus facilitated the establishment of several guerrilla training camps and of guerrilla command and control facilities, as well as a variety of propaganda and covert activities and the transportation of tons of weapons.

The evidence reveals that arms flowed into El Salvador from Nicaragua in preparation for the Salvadoran guerrillas' unsuccessful "final offensive" of January 1981. Air supply of arms to the Salvadoran guerrillas came from Nicaragua's Papalonal airfield, small boats smuggled arms across the Gulf of Fonseca, and indirect supply routes which involved the use of Costa Rican territory were developed by the Sandinistas. The evidence also indicates that the Salvadoran guerrilla headquarters in Nicaragua evolved into a sophisticated command and control center.

At this writing, there are reports that the Sandinistas have cut back on their support for insurgency in the region, although the evidence is far from clear. One explanation may be that the Salvadoran guerrillas have been able to obtain ample arms within El Salvador. Moreover, some evidence indicates that arms shipments to El Salvador from Nicaragua, although reduced, continue—particularly shipments of ammunition. In any event, nothing we are aware of would indicate that the Sandinistas' ultimate commitment to the cause of the Salvadoran guerrillas—or to the cause of armed revolution in the region—has diminished.

The Present Crisis

As we have seen, Central America's contemporary crisis has been a long time in the making. By the late 1970's, the increasingly dangerous configuration of historic poverty, social injustice, frustrated expectations, and closed political systems was suddenly exacerbated by world economic recession and by intensified foreign-promoted communist insurgency. And just as the economic collapse and political impasse offered an opportunity for the insurgents, the insurgency aggravated the economic and political crisis by spreading violence and fear. To varying degrees, but with many common elements, this crisis is reflected in the situation of each of the five Central American nations.

EL SALVADOR. Nowhere is the link between economic decline and insecurity more apparent than in El Salvador, once perhaps the leading beneficiary of the Central American Common Market. El Salvador today faces violence and destruction that threaten economic collapse. Planting and harvesting have been disrupted, buses and trucks burned, bridges and electric pylons dynamited. The cumulative direct cost of the war to the economy has been estimated at more than $600 million, with indirect costs far higher. El Salvador's economy is now less than three-quarters the size it was in 1978, and national income on a per capita basis is roughly at the level of the early 1960's.

The insurgents themselves acknowledge that destruction of the country's basic infrastructure is a key ingredient in their strategy to bring down the government. They seek victory through both economic and military attrition. Although their absolute numbers have not increased over the last three years, and although they have not attracted the broad popular support they hoped for, the guerrillas after four years of experience in the field demonstrate an increasing capacity to maneuver, concentrate their forces and attack selected targets. They maintain sporadic control over areas in the eastern provinces and pose a hit-and-run threat virtually everywhere outside the major urban areas. Guerrilla forces regularly attempt to intimidate and coerce local populations with shootings, abductions and other strong-arm tactics. And the human costs of the war have been immense. Displaced Salvadorans driven from their homes and leading a precarious existence within the country number in the hundreds of thousands. Many thousands more have left El Salvador as refugees.

On the other side, the Government of El Salvador is severely hampered by the erosion four years of war have produced in the country's basic institutions—by the difficulty it has in enforcing its authority and carrying out its functions. For their part, the armed forces have increased their manpower four-fold but still face problems in leadership and the command structure, as well as the need for more equipment and training. But the war effort suffers most of all from the terrible violence engulfing El Salvador's civilian population. Since 1979 more than 30,000 non-combatants have been killed. Government security forces and the right-wing death squads associated with them are guilty of many thousands of murders. These enemies of non-violent change above all threaten hopes for social and democratic reform.

There was little dispute among the witnesses appearing before the Commission that, in the words of one of them, "El Salvador needed a revolution"—a democratic revolution. The coup d'etat carried out by young officers in October of 1979 put an end to the brutal regime of General Romero and opened the way for that revolution. In the years since, even in the midst of escalating violence, the struggle for basic reform and a democratic transformation has continued. A sweeping program of land reform, now affecting 20 percent of the country's arable land, was launched; a Constituent Assembly election was held in which about 80 percent of those eligible went to the polls under very adverse circumstances; a new constitution has now been written and the country is preparing to elect a president in March.

[34]

GUATEMALA. Guatemala is also suffering from violence and economic decline. Its economy is the largest and most diversified in Central America. But it still depends on coffee exports for more than 60 percent of its agricultural foreign exchange earnings. With the decline in real prices for coffee during the last few years, the economic growth rates, quite satisfactory in the 1970's, turned negative. Insurgency and political violence dried up sources of international credit. Stagnation of the Central American Common Market, in which 80 percent of Guatemala's industrial exports are normally sold, hit the industrial sector hard. Gross national product fell by over 4 percent in 1983.

Guatemala's economic troubles affect a society long afflicted by the most extreme social inequity. Sanitation, potable water and proper shelter barely exist in the country's rural areas, where almost two-thirds of the population live. More than 50 percent of adults are illiterate, and life expectancy is less than 60 years. Overshadowing all social issues in Guatemala is the presence of a large and culturally distinct Indian population. Centuries of isolation and passivity are now giving way among the Indians to discontent and a drive to participate in Guatemala's economy and politics. Thus the crisis there takes on an extra dimension.

In 1982, young officers broke the political pattern of the past, overthrowing the brutal regime of General Lucas and installing a junta headed by the maverick General Efraín Ríos Montt, who subsequently named himself President. Under Ríos Montt the Guatemalan army made significant progress against the guerrilla forces, combining civic action with aggressive military action into a strategy of "beans and bullets." The government curbed the murderous activities of the security services in the cities, but set up secret tribunals with the power to give death sentences; and some rural areas were reportedly terrorized with killings designed to end local support for the guerrillas.

A new military regime, which replaced that of Ríos Montt last year, has scheduled constituent assembly elections for July of 1984, promised general elections for 1985 and announced that the armed forces will stay out of the political process.

With 20 years of experience in counter-insurgency, the Guatemalan army has so far been able to contain the guerrilla threat, despite the lack of outside assistance, and despite shortages of equipment and spare parts. But violence in the cities—terrorist attacks by the extreme left and the use of murder by the security services to repress dissent—is again growing. Insecurity thus spreads through the country.

NICARAGUA. In Nicaragua the revolution that overthrew the hated Somoza regime has been captured by self-proclaimed Marxist-Leninists. In July of 1979 the Sandinistas promised the OAS that they would organize "a truly democratic government" and hold free elections, but that promise has not been redeemed. Rather, the government has been brought fully under the control of the Sandinista National Directorate. Only two months after giving their pledge to the OAS and while successfully negotiating loans in Washington, the Sandinistas issued Decree No. 67, which converted their movement into the country's official political party and laid the foundation for the monopoly of political power they now enjoy. The Sandinista Directorate has progressively put in place a Cuban-style regime, complete with mass organizations under its political direction, an internal security system to keep watch on the entire population, and a massive military establishment. This comprehensive police and military establishment not only ensures the monopoly on power within Nicaragua, it also produces an acute sense of insecurity among Nicaragua's neighbors.

From the outset, the Sandinistas have maintained close ties with Cuba and the Soviet Union. There are some 8,000 Cuban advisers now in Nicaragua, including at least 2,000 military advisers, as well as several hundred Soviet, East European, Libyan and PLO advisers. Cuban construction teams have helped build military roads, bases and airfields. According to intelligence sources, an estimated 15,000 tons of Soviet bloc arms and equipment reached the Sandinista army in 1983. This military connection with Cuba, the Soviet Union, and its satellites internationalizes Central America's security problems and adds a menacing new dimension.

Nicaragua's government has made significant gains against illiteracy and disease. But despite significant U.S. aid from 1979 to 1981 (approximately $117 million), its economic performance has been poor, in part because of the disruptions caused by the revolution, in part because of the world recession, and in part because of the mismanagement invariably associated with regimes espousing Marxist-Leninist ideology. National income per capita is less than $1,000, about equal to that of the early 1960's, and Nicaragua is plagued by shortages of food and consumer goods, with the result that extensive rationing has been instituted.

Under military pressure from Nicaraguan rebels who reportedly receive U.S. support, and under diplomatic pressure from the international community, especially from the Contadora group, the Sandinistas have recently promised to announce early this year a date and rules for 1985 elections; have offered a partial amnesty to the anti-Sandinista guerrillas; have claimed a relaxation of censorship on *La Prensa*, the only opposition newspaper; have entered into talks with the Roman Catholic hierarchy; and have issued proposals for regional security agreements. In addition, reports from Sandinista sources in Managua have hinted at a permanently reduced Cuban presence and of diminished support to other Marxist-Leninist revolutionary groups in Central America—although we have no confirmation that either has taken place or is likely to take place. Whether any one of these moves reflects a true change of course or merely tactical maneuvers remains to be seen.

HONDURAS. Honduras borders Nicaragua and believes itself threatened by the Sandinistas' highly militarized and radically revolutionary regime. In Honduras an elected government is struggling to preserve security and maintain a democratic order established just two years ago after the military backed a return to constitutional, civilian rule. The government is also struggling to restore economic growth in the face of what President Roberto Suazo has called the worst economic crisis in the nation's history. The Sandinista military buildup—huge by Central American standards—puts heavy pressure on Honduras to strengthen its own forces at the expense of its development needs. The clandestine transshipment of arms from Nicaragua across Honduran territory and over the Bay of Fonseca traps Honduras in the bitter conflict of its neighbor.

The Suazo government has pursued national security through closer military ties with the United States and by supporting anti-Sandinista guerrillas operating from Honduran territory, reportedly in cooperation with the U.S. Honduras has rejected Nicaraguan proposals that such issues as border security and arms trafficking be addressed on a bilateral basis, insisting that a comprehensive regional political settlement, including an unmistakable commitment to democratic pluralism by all five countries, is essential if peace is to be restored.

Honduras's economy is highly dependent on coffee and banana exports and has suffered severely in recent years from the weakness in the international commodity markets. High rates of economic growth in the late 1970's have been reversed. Gross domestic product grew by less than 1 per cent in 1981 and declined by 2.5 percent the following year. According to the government's own figures, 57 percent of Honduras's families live in extreme poverty, unable to pay the cost of the basic basket of food. Population has been growing by an extraordinary 3.4 percent annually, and 48 percent are below the age of 15. The mixture of extreme poverty, high unemployment, steadily deteriorating social conditions and a very young population is potentially explosive.

COSTA RICA. In Costa Rica a long-established democratic order remains healthy, but the nation's economy is in distress and Costa Ricans are increasingly concerned that the violence in the region will intrude on their hitherto peaceful oasis. The international recession and the stagnation of the Central American Common Market caused a severe economic decline. National income per capita fell by 18 percent between 1980 and 1982. Unemployment doubled. Deterioration in the country's trade balance—in large part due to the drop in coffee prices and the rise in oil prices—led to heavy international borrowing. Costa Rica's foreign debt is now over $3 billion. Interest payments alone that were due in 1983 came to $500 million, or 58 percent of anticipated export receipts; arrears currently stand at $1 billion.

The government of President Luis Alberto Monge has responded seriously, adopting a severe austerity program, raising taxes, increasing fuel prices and public utility charges and freezing government employment. Efforts have been made to establish a realistic exchange rate, to cut public sector spending and bring the finances of autonomous agencies under central government control. However, the Monge administration is committed to maintaining the social and educational programs that have been so important in the nation's development. These programs have contributed to a 90 percent literacy rate and a life expectancy of 73 years—among the best figures for those categories in all of Latin America.

On its visit to Costa Rica, the Commission found great anxiety about the situation in Nicaragua. Costa Rica has no armed forces beyond a small civil guard and rural constabulary. A dispute with Nicaragua over navigation on the San Juan River and the operations of anti-Sandinista guerrillas in the area have created a high degree of tension along the northern border. Sandinista and Cuban propaganda campaigns vilifying their country, and Sandinista political and intelligence operations there, have alarmed Costa Ricans. On November 10, 1983, President Monge declared strict military neutrality in Central America's conflicts, making clear that his government intended to remain unarmed and to continue to rely on international agreements for its security. But he also made clear that Costa Rica will not be neutral politically as between "democracy and totalitarianism."

THE COMMON DANGERS. Although the current situation differs substantially from country to country, there are many common elements.

The region as a whole has suffered severe economic setbacks. All five nations are markedly poorer than they were just a few years ago. Intra-regional trade has fallen drastically. The Common Market is threatened with extinction as the resources necessary to sustain it dry up. Political violence and the menace of the radical left have caused huge flights of capital. Investment, even in the leading agricultural export sectors, has come virtually to an end.

The tragedy of the homeless is one of the most bitter fruits of Central America's conflict. Although no accurate count of refugees and displaced persons is available, the Commission received estimates of up to one million Central Americans who have left their homes: Nicaraguans moving into Costa Rica and Honduras to escape the oppression of the Sandinistas; Guatemalan Indians fleeing into Mexico from the conflict in the highlands; Salvadorans seeking safety in Honduras, or a better life in the United States. But those who must endure the worst conditions are the displaced, driven from their homes but unable to seek refuge in another land.

Other costs are also evident. According to testimony before the Commission, health, nutrition and educational services that were already badly deficient are declining further. Unemployment and underemployment are spreading—an overriding social and economic problem in all five countries. The high rate of population growth magnifies these problems. Job opportunities are vanishing, even as a quarter of a million young people are entering Central America's job markets each year. In a region where half of the population is below the age of 20, the combination of youth and massive unemployment is a problem of awesome—and explosive—dimensions.

The configuration of economic recession, political turbulence and foreign intervention makes the crisis in Central America both exceptionally difficult and exceptionally ominous. Although turmoil has often accompanied economic difficulty in Central America, it has never before been so calculated to create chaos and want. This both intensifies the conflict and accelerates the economic and political decay of the region.

The prospect of even greater calamaties should not be underestimated. None of the five Central American states is free of war or the threat of war. As the conflicts intensify, and as Nicaragua builds an armed force with firepower vastly greater than anything ever seen before in Central America, the threat of militarization hangs over the region. Were this to happen, it could further warp Central America's societies and shut off the possibilities for internal and external accommodations.

The United States and Central America

HISTORICAL PERSPECTIVE. The United States has been involved, sometimes intimately, in the affairs of Central America for more than a century. The record of that past is a mixed one; it must be understood if we are to address today's crisis constructively.

After the 1848 war with Mexico, the United States developed a keen interest in opening a secure transportation route to its new territories on the Pacific. It took that era's sailing ships no less than three months to get from New York to California. A canal through Central America would serve both safety and speed. At first, Nicaragua seemed a particularly favorable site. The canal was eventually built in Panama more than half a century later, after President Theodore Roosevelt secured U.S. rights to the Canal Zone by helping to arrange a coup that established Panama's independence from Colombia. But it was interest in a canal that first spurred U.S. involvement in Nicaragua and the isthmus.

For the most part, U.S. policy toward Central America during the early part of this century focused primarily on promoting the stability and solvency of local governments so as to keep other nations out. This was reflected in Theodore Roosevelt's Corollary to the Monroe Doctrine, which held that the United States should take action to prevent situations from arising that might lead to interventions by extra-hemispheric powers. Theodore Roosevelt once defined the sole desire of the United States as being "to see all neighboring countries stable, orderly and prosperous." This formulation reflects both a great-power interest in keeping the hemisphere insulated from European intrigue and the concern for others' well-being that has often animated our foreign policy. The result, however, was a high degree of interventionism in Central America during the early 1900's.

The United States intervened directly in Nicaragua in 1909, landing Marines and deposing a president in an effort to restore stability. The Marines returned in 1912 and, with one brief interruption, they stayed until 1933. Before leaving, the U.S. authorities created a single National Guard with responsibility for all Nicaraguan police and defense functions. The immediate purpose was to provide stability; the ultimate result was to create the instrument Anastasio Somoza used after the occupation to impose a personal dictatorship once the Marines left. The ability of Somoza and later his sons to portray themselves as friends and even spokesmen of the U.S. began with the use they were able to make of the legacy of U.S. military occupation, thereby creating an identity between the U.S. and dictatorship in Central America that lingers, independent of the facts, to this day.

Besides military interventions, the U.S. used other forms of pressure as well. At various times these included customs receiverships, debt refundings, and non-recognition of governments that had come to power by force. None of these policies worked very well, and they aroused considerable resentment. In addition, private U.S. citizens sometimes engaged in free-wheeling operations of their own—such as an invasion of Nicaragua in the late 1850's by freebooter William Walker, or the financing of a revolution in Honduras in 1911 by Samuel Zemurray to protect his shipping and banana interests. The legacy of these private interventions also continues, understandably, to color the attitudes of many Central Americans towards the United States.

Franklin Roosevelt's Good Neighbor Policy was designed to signal the end of the era of intervention and to put relations with all of Latin America on a basis of mutual respect and friendship. But in practice—and particularly when World War II put an added premium on good relations with neighboring governments —this policy of friendship and non-intervention had the paradoxical effect of continuing to identify the United States with established dictatorships.

The importance of the United States to the region's economies has also been a powerful element in shaping Central American attitudes toward us. Beginning in Costa Rica almost a century ago, U.S. capital developed the banana industry and monopolized it throughout the isthmus. For decades, the United Fruit Company was known in the area as "the octopus." It controlled much of the region's transportation and communications. Bananas were vital to the economies of several countries, and United Fruit dominated the international markets for the fruit. Since the 1950's patterns of both land ownership and distribution in the banana industry have diversified. United Fruit itself no longer exists; its successor, United Brands, is widely regarded as both a model citizen and a model employer. But the questionable practices followed by the fruit companies in those early years, together with the power they wielded over weak governments, did a lot to create the fear of "economic imperialism" that to some degree still persists among Central Americans.

A HISTORY OF COOPERATION. This, however, is only one side of the history of U.S. relations with Central America. The U.S. government has also made extensive positive efforts to advance Central American development, beginning at the turn of the century with a public health campaign against yellow fever. During the Second World War the Institute of Inter-American Affairs, headed by Nelson Rockefeller, was established. The Institute developed a system of "Servicios"—bilateral organizations to finance and manage projects in health, education and housing. Through the decade of the 1950's the Servicios provided training and experience to a new generation of Central American technicians and professionals.

With the launching of the Alliance for Progress in 1961, the role of the United States in Central American development underwent a major transformation. This was a bold and unprecedented effort to encourage comprehensive national planning and to promote a wide array of social, political, tax and land reforms, supported by significantly increased resources from the United States, the newly created Inter-American Development Bank, the World Bank and other aid donors. The assistance from the United States, and perhaps equally as significant, the personal identification of President Kennedy with the program, was a critical factor in the surge of Central American development which began in the 1960's.

U.S. assistance was instrumental in the creation of effective central banks and private intermediate credit institutions, and in the establishment of agricultural cooperatives, housing projects, roads, health centers, population assistance, and technical training. The Alliance for Progress also provided major funding and cooperative planning to the Central American Common Market, which was perhaps its most important single contribution to Central American growth during this period.

In essence, the Alliance was a compact between our government and the governments of Latin America. The goals of the Alliance were three: economic growth, structural change in societies, and political democratization. But as we have seen, it was only in the first area that significant progress was made. Central America's growth rate of over 5 percent per capita during the 1960's far surpassed the 2.5 percent target for all of Latin America laid down in the charter of the Alliance. An impressive inventory of physical infrastructure was constructed in the five Central American countries during this period, including schools, hospitals, low-cost housing, and sewage systems.

But the other two goals of the Alliance, structural change and political democratization, proved much more difficult to achieve.

Direct private investment in Central America by U.S. firms also continued to grow during these years. While that investment might seem small in relation to total U.S. investment abroad (currently about 2.4 percent, including Panama), it was large in Central American terms. It has contributed substantially to the region's growth, as many Central Americans are quick to acknowledge. At the same time, it has been a constant target of the propaganda of the radical left, which has played upon the theme of economic hegemony and "imperialism."

Central America's dependence on trade with the United States has, of course, always been high. Though the portion of the region's exports that came to the United States declined from 61 percent in 1955 to 36 percent in 1975, the U.S. still led all other countries as a market for Central American products and commodities. While such dependence remains a sensitive issue, investment from the U.S. and trade relations with the U.S. are critically important to the economies of Central America.

MIXED RESULTS. The record of United States involvement in Central America during these critical years is, in short, mixed. The Alliance for Progress was a major force for modernization and development. U.S. assistance programs have made and continue to make an important contribution. Whatever the mistakes of the past, private U.S. investment in the region now plays a vital and constructive role.

It may be that U.S. diplomacy gave too little attention to the growing problems in Central America during the past two decades. Certainly, the U.S. has at times been insensitive, at times interfering, at times preoccupied elsewhere. This is a far cry, however, from saying, as the Sandinista National Directorate and others say, that this nation's policies have been the principal cause of the region's afflictions.

U.S. Interests in the Crisis

When strategic interests conflict with moral interests, the clash presents one of the classic challenges to confront societies and statesman. But in Central America today, our strategic and moral interests coincide. We shall deal later in the report with the specifics of those interests. But in broad terms they must include:

- To preserve the moral authority of the United States. To be perceived by others as a nation that does what is right *because* it is right is one of this country's principal assets.
- To improve the living conditions of the people of Central America. They are neighbors. Their human need is tinder waiting to be ignited. And if it is, the conflagration could threaten the entire hemisphere.
- To advance the cause of democracy, broadly defined, within the hemisphere.
- To strengthen the hemispheric system by strengthening what is now, in both economic and social terms, one of its weakest links.
- To promote peaceful change in Central America while resisting the violation of democracy by force and terrorism.
- To prevent hostile forces from seizing and expanding control in a strategically vital area of the Western Hemisphere.
- To bar the Soviet Union from consolidating either directly or through Cuba a hostile foothold on the American continents in order to advance its strategic purposes.

In short, the crisis in Central America is of large and acute concern to the United States because Central America is our near neighbor and a strategic crossroads of global significance; because Cuba and the Soviet Union are investing heavily in efforts to expand their footholds there, so as to carry out designs for the hemisphere distinctly hostile to U.S. interests; and because the people of Central America are sorely beset and urgently need our help.

The Future

We think this challenge can—and must—be met. The Commission takes heart in the refusal of Central Americans to succumb to despair. Everywhere we found hope for a democratic future and a readiness to sacrifice toward that end. The high level of sustained economic growth during the postwar period demonstrates that Central America has the human and material resources to develop rapidly. The region's leaders, both in government and in the private sector, expressed their understanding that there must be greater equity in the distribution of economic benefits and greater justice in social relations. If that understanding is translated into reality, the opportunity for more balanced and sustained development should be at hand.

We shall discuss in a later chapter what can be done to revive the economies of the region. Let us simply note here that the small size of these countries means that significant but not vast amounts of outside assistance can make an important difference —and that with such assistance Central America can progress.

The people of Central America have lived too long with poverty, deprivation and violence. The current turmoil must not be allowed to shatter their hopes for a brighter future.

They have endured too many generations of misrule to let their aspirations for democratic political development be dashed in this generation on the rocks of fear, division and violence. Not least, their own security—and ours—must no longer be threatened by hostile powers which seek expansion of influence through exploitation of misery.

The crisis, thus, poses an urgent challenge to the United States. But that challenge in turn presents us with an opportunity —an opportunity to help the people of Central America translate their dreams of a better and a freer life into reality.

CHAPTER 4

TOWARD DEMOCRACY AND ECONOMIC PROSPERITY

THE CRISIS in Central America has no single, simple cause, but the troubled performance of the region's economies has been a major factor. They were among the most dynamic in the world during the 1960's and early 1970's. But that growth was unevenly distributed and poverty continued to plague most of the region's people. As the Final Document of the Catholic Conference of Latin American Bishops at Puebla, Mexico recognized in 1979, there was a "growing gap between rich and poor," which the conference characterized as a "contradiction of Christian existence." This contributed to a growing political frustration in several countries, intensified by the fact that some sectors of these societies were enjoying economic success.

Then, in the late 1970's, production, export earnings, incomes, profits, and consumption all began to decline. The result was a sharp economic contraction in each country of the region. The effects have been particularly severe for those who were denied participation in the earlier era of rapid growth.

Yet our meetings with the leaders and people of Central America and our consideration of the facts put before us during the hearings have convinced us that the Central American economies can grow again, and that the fruits of that growth can be more equitably shared. This will require that:

- Economic growth goes forward in tandem with social and political modernization.
- Indigenous savings are encouraged and supplemented by substantial external aid.

- The nations of the region pursue appropriate economic policies.
- In particular, these policies recognize that success will ultimately depend on the reinvigoration of savings, growth, and employment.

The program the Commission envisions—aimed at promoting democratization, economic growth, human development and security—would break new ground. Most past U.S. development programs have been predominately economic. We argue here that the crisis in Central America cannot be considered in solely economic or political or social or security terms. The requirements for the development of Central America are a seamless web. The actions we recommend represent an attempt to address this complex interrelationship in its totality, not just in its parts.

This chapter focuses on broad issues of economic performance, recovery and expansion. We propose specific programs to reinvigorate critical elements within the Central American economies in conjunction with social and political change and progress. We envision, in the short term, an emergency stabilization program and, in the medium and long term, a new multilateral regional organization to measure performance across the entire political, social, economic, and security spectrum, and to target external aid resources where they can provide the most significant impetus. In support of these efforts, we urge a five-year commitment by the United States to a substantially increased level of economic assistance.

We recognize that large-scale economic aid alone does not guarantee progress. The most successful growth efforts in the postwar period—including Central America's own sustained expansion during the 1960's and 1970's—were led by the private sector. In these cases governments provided appropriate incentives and eliminated roadblocks, rather than trying to make themselves the engines of growth. This must be done again in Central America.

Success will turn in part on the ability of the nations of Central America to take full advantage of the enterprise, courage, and initiative of individuals and of non-governmental institutions and groups: businesses, voluntary organizations, the churches and their lay organizations, trade unions, agriculture and peasant leaders and cooperatives. All these have roles to play.

We recognize that it is unlikely that the social inequities and distortions that have accumulated over the last five centuries will be corrected during the next five years. But the groundwork for recovery should be laid as soon as possible. To that end, bold initiatives are needed. The costs of not meeting the challenge in Central America would be too great, today and for generations to come.

CURRENT ECONOMIC CONDITIONS
AND THEIR CAUSES

Before presenting our policy recommendations, we turn first to an examination of current economic conditions and of the causes of the crisis. Adverse international economic and financial developments, natural disasters, ineffective economic policies within Central America, structural economic weaknesses, and high levels of violence have combined to produce inflation, a decline in economic activity, capital flight, and problems in servicing debt. The results have imposed particularly grim burdens on the poor.

GDP Decline from Peak Year Through 1983

	GDP	Peak Year	GDP per capita	Peak Year
El Salvador	−25%	1978	−35%	1978
Honduras	− 2%	1981	−12%	1979
Costa Rica	−15%	1980	−23%	1979
Guatemala	− 7%	1981	−14%	1980
Nicaragua	−22%	1977	−38%	1977

By 1983 real per capita income in Nicaragua was 38% below the peak level reached in 1977; the contraction in El Salvador was 35%. Costa Rica (−23%), Guatemala (−14%) and Honduras (−12%) have also suffered. Another way of looking at the economic decline is to note that in Costa Rica, Guatemala, and Honduras the absolute levels of real per capita income today barely equal those of the mid 1970's. In El Salvador and Nicaragua real per capita income has fallen to the levels of the early 1960's.

The pattern of export-led growth that characterized regional economic development in the 1960's and 1970's resulted in economies which are highly sensitive to world economic conditions, as well as highly interdependent. An economic shock in one country affects all. This is particularly true of the five members of the Central American Common Market—Costa Rica, El Salvador, Guatemala, Honduras, and Nicaragua. They developed a strong trade among themselves in manufactured goods and developed much of their economic infrastructure (e.g., transportation and power systems) on a regional basis. One result is that, despite the political differences dividing the region, Nicaragua remains an essential part of the Central American economy, although the pronounced deterioration in that country over the last several years has undermined some of the linkages with the rest of the region.

The contraction of the past several years has led to higher levels of unemployment and underemployment, and increased poverty. According to the Economic Commission for Latin America, more than one-third of the region's population lacks sufficient income to purchase a nutritionally adequate diet. The consequences are poor health conditions, inadequate nutrition, deficient education, and the other social problems described in the next chapter.

Continued rapid population growth has compounded the human consequences of the economic collapse. The population of the Central American isthmus nearly doubled from 1960 to 1981, from 12 to 23 million. During these years, population growth rates slowed significantly only in Costa Rica and Panama. Overall, the regional growth rate remains around 3 percent, among the highest in the world. Current projections are for a regional population of 38 million in the year 2000, with population growth averaging 2.7 percent per year; at that rate, the population would double in 26 years.

[50]

CAUSES OF THE RECENT DECLINE

Although the economies of the region were once among the most dynamic in the world, they are now in decline. This painful change can be attributed to several factors:

High oil prices, world inflation, prolonged world recession, and weak demand and prices for commodity exports

All of the countries in the region were badly affected by the sharp rise in oil prices during the 1970's. Oil imports in 1981, after the second round of price rises and before the collapse of Central America's exports, cost more than one-fifth of export revenues. The high cost of energy imports is a continuing problem. Slack world demand for Central America's key export products (coffee, bananas, cotton, sugar, and meat) led to a drastic deterioration of the region's purchasing power. As a result, Central America would have to export in physical terms almost half again as much today as it did five years ago to buy the same goods on the world market. The shortfall in export earnings forced the Central American countries to cut back imports not only of consumer goods, but also of raw materials, spare parts, and capital goods, thus accelerating the economic slowdown.

Intra-regional tensions and political unrest

The conflict between El Salvador and Honduras in 1969 began a process which gradually undermined the dynamics of the Central American Common Market. Nevertheless, intra-regional trade, largely in manufactured goods, continued to grow until 1980. Since then the political turmoil in Nicaragua and El Salvador, and the financial problems of all the CACM countries have produced a sharp decline in intra-regional trade: the value of such trade fell by almost one-third between 1980 and 1982. This collapse of intra-CACM trade—in part because of the accumulation of serious trade imbalances between Costa Rica and Guatemala, which had surpluses, and Nicaragua, El Salvador, and Honduras, which had deficits—contributed to region-wide economic contraction.

As well as damaging the economic infrastructure, political

conflicts led to retrenchment by commercial banks and investors. Private sector confidence, both within and outside Central America, has been shaken; domestic and foreign investment has declined; and capital flight has been substantial—perhaps as much as $3 billion over the last several years. These developments have seriously undermined the prospects for future growth.

Economic management

In the past, Central American countries generally pursued relatively sound economic policies, which contributed to strong growth and low inflation through the 1960's and much of the 1970's. But in the late 1970's, unsuccessful attempts to sustain domestic economic activity in the face of the second oil shock, the sharp increase in international interest rates, and the onset of recession in the United States led to high budget deficits, excessive monetary growth, and sharply higher foreign debt in almost all of these countries. In some cases government policies resulted in disincentives, including inappropriate tax policies, which penalized investment and export activity. The results contributed to higher inflation (especially in Costa Rica, where consumer prices rose 90 percent in 1982), declining investment, and economic contraction.

Excessive foreign debt

One of the legacies of the past several years is a significant accumulation of external debt. Total debt of the Central American countries was at least $14 billion at the end of 1982, an increase of 240% over 1975. The size of the debt and the burden of servicing it are highest in Costa Rica, Nicaragua, and Panama. In Costa Rica, total external debt equals more than 140% of Gross Domestic Product (GDP) and scheduled debt service (interest and term amortization payments) account for more than one-half of export earnings. In Panama and Nicaragua foreign debt is equal to around 75% and 100% of GDP, respectively, and scheduled debt service equals about one-third of foreign earnings in both countries.

Although the burden of these debts and their service is less than in some other countries in the Western Hemisphere, all of the nations of Central America are having difficulty in maintain-

[52]

ing timely debt-service payments. Several countries have already rescheduled part of their external debt, and others are in the process of doing so. Faced with these conditions, all of the Central American countries—except Nicaragua—have adopted economic stabilization programs sanctioned by the International Monetary Fund (IMF). These programs aim at reducing inflation, stabilizing the balance of payments, and re-creating the conditions for future economic growth. Unfortunately, in the short run the programs seem to be more successful in achieving the first two of these than in halting economic decline.

With the beginning of the international debt crisis, the Central American countries lost their limited access to the international commercial banking market. Trade finance lines were cut and public and private sector borrowers were unable to raise new funds, thus further compounding debt-service problems. To some extent, this reinforced the drop in imports and the decline in economic activity, even though increased official assistance more than offset the decline in commercial bank credits. Any program of reactivation must address these key factors. They lie at the heart of the region's development problems.

EFFORTS TO ADDRESS THE CRISIS

The Central Americans, the United States, and others are already making substantial efforts, thus preventing an even more serious deterioration in living conditions. The Central Americans —as they must—are bearing the largest part of the burden. Exacting economic stabilization programs are now being implemented in almost all of these countries, while further ambitious budget, monetary, pricing, and institutional reforms are being considered. In addition, governments are beginning to provide incentives to encourage investment as well as extra-regional trade. Volunteer groups, especially religious and lay organizations, are providing valuable social welfare services which governments are unable to finance because of budgetary constraints.

For their part, other countries are also contributing to Central America's economic recuperation. Mexico and Venezuela have established a major facility to provide oil on concessional terms. The United States is making its influence felt in several ways:

- By its own economic recovery, which should eventually be reflected in greater demand and better prices for Central American exports.
- By the Caribbean Basin Initiative (CBI), which opens up favorable prospects for new Central American trade, and by the Generalized System of Preferences (GSP), which extends duty free access to the U.S. market for many Central American products.
- By its bilateral economic assistance programs, which have been considerably expanded during the last few years and, for the region as whole, totalled $628 million in the last fiscal year.
- By its contribution to multilateral agencies, including the Inter-American Development Bank, the International Monetary Fund, and the World Bank, which in turn provide financial support, policy advice, and technical assistance.
- By its support of the international coffee agreement.
- By the initiative of the thousands of United States private citizens working in voluntary organizations and on their own to help improve living conditions in the region.

But the outlook, even under optimistic assumptions, is not very promising. Even if economic stabilization policies are consistently implemented, if official capital flows remain at roughly current levels through the rest of the decade, if private capital flows eventually recover, if the international economic environment gradually improves, and if political stability returns, unless more is done the economies of Central America will only gradually begin to recover. The decline has been so sharp over the past several years that any economic recovery would probably remain fragile, even if all the conditions already outlined were met. Without a significant increase in the levels of foreign assistance, improvement in the way those resources are managed and used, and the introduction of growth-oriented economic policies, economic activity in the region, measured on a per capita basis, would probably reach no more than three-quarters of the 1980 level by 1990. This would mean more unemployment and continued widespread poverty.

In short, present prospects for Central America are unacceptable and the present effort is inadequate. The Central American countries must improve their own economic policies and performance. The United States and the other democracies must provide more assistance and greater commitment. Central America needs additional resources to finance new investments, to rebuild its productive capacity, to utilize more fully existing capacity, to replace damaged infrastructure, and to maintain debt service. The latter is essential to restoring international financial credibility.

We therefore turn to the specific elements of what must be done.

AN EMERGENCY STABILIZATION PROGRAM

We cannot wait to check the decline in economic activity and the deterioration in social conditions until a long-term program is in place. The Commission therefore urges the immediate adoption of an emergency stabilization program combining public and private efforts to halt the deterioration. Some of our recommendations are endorsements of existing initiatives. And, most important, it is critical that the Central American countries continue to implement economic stabilization programs and, especially, to pursue policies designed to foster increased investment and trade.

The program includes eight key elements:

We urge that the leaders of the United States and the Central American countries meet to initiate a comprehensive approach to the economic development of the region and the reinvigoration of the Central American Common Market.

The United States and the Central American countries should convene a conference this year to discuss the impediments to and opportunities for economic, political and social development. The agenda for such a meeting should include consideration of efforts to reinvigorate the Central American Common Market, the role of the foreign and domestic private sectors in seeking economic recovery, and the promotion of balanced regional and hemispheric trade. In addition, as discussed later in this chapter, we recommend that the leaders consider a new multilateral organization to promote comprehensive regional devlopment.

We encourage the greatest possible involvement of the private sector in the stabilization effort.

Renewed investment and lending, higher production from existing facilities, more training, increased purchases of Central American goods, and other initiatives would provide immediate economic benefits. Health care professionals, educators, labor officials, churchmen and women, and others can provide and are providing much needed training and technical advice. Some of the government programs described below are designed to encourage even greater private sector efforts.

We recognize that the current climate of violence and uncertainty discourages private sector initiatives. Nevertheless, we believe it is imperative to increase the private sector's involvement as soon as possible. Thus, we recommend the establishment of an Emergency Action Committee of concerned private citizens and organizations with a mandate to provide advice on the development of new public-private initiatives to spur growth and employment in the region.

We recommend that the United States actively address the external debt problems of the region.

We urge new initiatives to deal with Central America's serious external debt problems. Although the United States and other creditor governments have agreed in principle to reschedule part of Costa Rica's external debt, none of the other countries of the region has formally asked for similar treatment. They should be encouraged to seek multilateral debt renegotiation; this would be a departure from existing practice which is essentially reactive.

At the same time, the United States and the governments of other creditor countries should urge private lenders, especially commercial banks, to renegotiate existing debt at the lowest possible interest rates. A task force of key public and private creditors as well as debtors could be established to facilitate these debt renegotiations and to encourage new lending. The task force could establish general guidelines for individual country negotiations and do everything possible to expedite agreement between debtors and creditors. Again, the engagement of creditor governments would be a significant departure from current approaches.

We do not intend that our recommendations should affect the debt negotiations of countries outside of Central America, but we believe that the debt burden needs to be addressed as part of the emergency stabilization effort.

We recommend that the United States provide an immediate increase in bilateral economic assistance.

Additional economic assistance should be made available in the current fiscal year. Total commitments of U.S. bilateral economic assistance to Belize, Costa Rica, El Salvador, Guatemala, Honduras, Nicaragua, and Panama in FY 1983 was $628 million; the request for appropriated funds for FY 1984 is $477 million. We recommend a supplemental appropriation of $400 million for the current fiscal year. Such an increase, if complemented by continued improvements in the economic policy programs of these countries and if quickly made available, would help stabilize current economic conditions. (Forecasts of the financial needs of the region are summarized in the appendix to this chapter.) We also recommend additional U.S. economic assistance in future years, which is discussed in the proposed medium-term program.

The bulk of this additional assistance should be channeled through the Agency for International Development (AID), with emphasis on creating productive jobs, providing general balance of payments support, and helping the recipient countries implement their economic stabilization programs. The purpose of this assistance would be to stop the continued decline in economic activity, and to signal a U.S. commitment to helping Central America address its deep-seated economic and political problems. Other donors, including Canada, Europe and Japan should be encouraged to provide similar additional help as soon as possible.

[57]

We recommend that a major thrust of expanded aid should be in labor intensive infrastructure and housing projects.

Although the housing needs of the region are addressed in the next chapter, we urge that AID use increased economic assistance to expand infrastructure and housing projects. Central America suffers from pressing needs for rural electrification, irrigation, roads, bridges, municipal water, sewer and drainage construction and repair. Such construction projects, using labor-intensive methods, can quickly be initiated, with considerable economic benefit.

We recommend that new official trade credit guarantees be made available to the Central American countries.

The decline in the availability of trade finance has critically affected the flow of imports into Central America. A Trade Credit Insurance Program would provide U.S. government guarantees for short-term trade credit from U.S. commercial banks. Such a program could be administered by the Export-Import Bank, although the existing trade credit program is not available to Central American countries, in part because the risks of non-repayment are viewed as excessive. Therefore, every effort should be made to establish the program within existing legislation or to create new legislative authority for a program reflecting the need for special consideration in Central America. The novelty would be that the program would be available only for use in Central America.

We further recommend that participating U.S. commercial banks be required, as a condition of their participation, to re-negotiate their existing long-term credits in accordance with guidelines established by the debt task force described above. Thus, the program would contribute to easing debt service problems as well as to encouraging renewed commercial bank lending (albeit with a government guarantee) in Central America.

We also urge that a program be organized to provide seasonal credit to the agricultural sector which would meet a critical need in the region.

We recommend that the United States provide an emergency credit to the Central American Common Market Fund (CACMF).

The Central American countries have asked for a credit to refinance part of the accumulated trade deficits among themselves which have contributed to the contraction of intra-regional trade. The United States should use part of the increased economic aid for this purpose; the Central American countries that have been in surplus would be expected to transform the remainder of the deficits into long-term local currency credits. As the Central American countries have proposed, CACMF regulations should then be adjusted to avoid future build-ups of large unsettled balances. Since the debts that would be refinanced under this proposal are among central banks, there should be no adverse implications for other rescheduling efforts.

We recognize that support for Common Market institutions benefits all members of the Common Market, regardless of their political orientation or social and economic performance. There is no way to isolate one or two member countries. However, support for the Common Market would be one of the quickest ways to revive intra-regional trade and economic activity. Historically, economic integration has had important political and economic benefits for the members of CACM, and the Common Market continues to enjoy strong support among Central Americans.

It is on this basis that we have concluded that the benefits of an infusion of capital into the CACMF outweigh the disadvantages. However, we are convinced that the Common Market will have to change toward a more open trading posture. This will require, as many Central American experts have suggested to us, a basic reorientation of regional trade and industrial policies.

We recommend that the United States join the Central American Bank for Economic Integration (CABEI).

The Central American countries are opening membership in CABEI to countries outside the region. We urge the U.S. to join this institution and to encourage other creditor countries to seek membership. The infusion of new resources would help reinvigorate the bank, which could channel much-needed funds to small-scale entrepreneurs and farmers, provide working capital to existing private sector companies, and encourage the development of new industries. Again, U.S. membership in CABEI would benefit all members of the Common Market.

A MEDIUM- AND LONG-TERM RECONSTRUCTION AND DEVELOPMENT PROGRAM

The measures we have outlined above aim at short-term stabilization. Essentially, they are emergency economic measures made necessary by the severity of the economic downturn. They represent an effort to buy time to permit the Central American nations and their friends to build a broader structure of cooperation for the longer future. That longer-term future is our principal mandate, and we now turn to it.

We have already expressed our conviction that political, social, and economic development goals must be addressed simultaneously. We have neither the responsibility nor the competence to design specific long-term development plans for each Central American country. These are for the Central Americans themselves. Nevertheless, we are obliged to define medium-term objectives which are compatible with the interests of the United States:

- *Elimination of the climate of violence and civil strife.*

Peace is an essential condition of economic and social progress. So too is elimination of the fear of brutality inflicted by arbitrary authority or terrorism. No need is more basic.

- *Development of democratic institutions and processes.*

The United States should encourage the Central American nations to develop and nurture democratic cultures, institutions, and practices, including:

- Strong judicial systems to enhance the capacity to redress grievances concerning personal security, property rights, and free speech.

- Free elections, by seeking advice from technical experts and studying successful electoral systems, including Costa Rica's.
- Free and democratic trade unions. The importance of unions, which represent millions of rural and urban workers, has been firmly established in the region. They have been not only an economic force but a political one as well, opposing arbitrary rule and promoting democratic values. Labor unions will continue to have an important part to play in political development, as well as in improving the social and economic well-being of working men and women. Assuring an equitable distribution of economic benefits will require both job-oriented development strategies and trade unions to protect workers' rights.

- *Development of strong and free economies with diversified production for both external and domestic markets.*

During the second half of this decade the Central American economies need to grow at per capita annual rates of at least 3 percent in real terms, which is close to the region's historical growth rate and is necessary to absorb new entrants to the labor force each year. This is an ambitious but realistic goal despite today's depressed conditions and the misfortunes of the recent past.

- *Sharp improvement in the social conditions of the poorest Central Americans.*

No investment in Central America will be more productive over the long term than that made to improve the health, education, and social welfare of its people. This is fundamental. We devote the next chapter to it.

- *Substantially improved distribution of income and wealth.*

The goals of equality of opportunity and better income distribution require expanded access to ownership of productive land and capital. This is also crucial for social and political progress. The pervasiveness and depth of rural poverty make improvement in rural incomes and living standards especially high priorities. Agrarian reform programs should continue to be pursued as means of achieving this.

These are ambitious goals. Their achievement will depend primarily on the policies adopted by the Central Americans themselves. As we have noted, efforts are already under way to achieve them. However, these efforts need to be expanded and enhanced; more important, they now lack the focus and framework necessary to signal a forceful, persistent, and long-term partnership committed to development, equity, and democracy in Central America.

Our recommendations are divided into two groups. The first of these involves proposals for U.S. public and private support for Central American development efforts. The second is a proposal for developing a new multilateral approach to address the region's comprehensive development needs.

The Nature of U.S. Development Support

We urge a major increase in U.S. and other country financial and economic assistance for Central America.

Unless there is a substantial increase in aid, in our view, the prospects for recovery are bleak. The solution to the crisis of Central America does not lie along the path of austerity. We believe that the people of the region must at a minimum perceive a reasonable prospect that, with sustained effort on their part, they can reach 1980 levels of per capita economic activity by no later than 1990, and, with determination and luck, well before that. However, as we have repeatedly stressed, unless economic recovery is accompanied by social progress and political reform, additional financial support will ultimately be wasted. By the same token, without recovery, the political and security prospects will be grim.

Reaching that goal will require a significant effort. External financing needs between now and 1990 have been estimated at as much as $24 billion for the seven countries as a group. (Forecasts are summarized in the appendix.) The World Bank, the International Monetary Fund, the Inter-American Development Bank, other official creditors, private investors, and commercial banks are likely to provide at least half of these funds—especially if each Central American country follows prudent economic policies, if there is steady social and political progress, and if outside aggression is eliminated. The balance, as much as $12 billion, would have to be supplied by the United States. (As defined in the appendix, this total financing need includes the projected financing requirements of Nicaragua, which is not now a recipient of U.S. assistance.)

We have already proposed that U.S. economic assistance be increased in FY 1984 to cover part of this on an emergency basis.

We now propose that economic assistance over the five-year period beginning in 1985 total $8 billion. Although the macroeconomic forecasts on which we base this proposal do not translate precisely into fiscal year federal budget requests, this global figure would include direct appropriations as well as contingent liabilities such as guarantees and insurance. In effect, this would represent a rough doubling of U.S. economic assistance from the 1983 level.

We recognize that such a proposal, at a time of serious concern in the United States about the level of governmental spending and the prospective size of the federal budget deficit, may be viewed with scepticism. However, we firmly believe that without such large-scale assistance, economic recovery, social progress, and the development of democratic institutions in Central America will be set back.

Because of the magnitude of the effort required and the importance of a long-term commitment, we further urge that Congress appropriate funds for Central America on a multiple-year basis. We strongly recommend a five-year authorization of money, a portion of which would be channelled through the proposed Central American Development Organization, which is outlined later in this chapter. The balance would support economic assistance programs administered by existing U.S. government agencies.

Ultimately, the effectiveness of increased economic assistance will turn on the economic policies of the Central American countries themselves. As we have noted, most have begun to move away from some of the policies which contributed to the current crisis. However, we agree with what many experts have

[63]

told us: that unless these reforms are extended economic performance will not significantly improve, regardless of the money foreign donors and creditors provide. In too many other countries, increased availability of financial resources has undermined reform by relieving the immediate pressure on policy makers. This must be avoided in Central America.

What is now required is a firm commitment by the Central American countries to economic policies, including reforms in tax systems, to encourage private enterprise and individual initiative, to create favorable investment climates, to curb corruption where it exists, and to spur balanced trade. These can lay the foundation for sustained growth.

The increased economic assistance we propose should be used to promote democracy, renew economic growth, improve living conditions, achieve better distribution of income and wealth, encourage more dynamic and open economies, and develop more productive agriculture. Specific programs are primarily the responsibilities of the recipient countries themselves. However, we strongly urge that the United States actively work to develop and nurture democratic institutions in the region.

We recommend that the United States expand economic assistance for democratic institutions and leadership training.

Key initiatives which either are already under way or should be developed include:

- The encouragement of neighborhood groups, community improvement organizations, and producer cooperatives which provide a training ground for democratic participation and help make governments more responsive to citizen demands.
- The United States Information Service's binational centers provide valuable insight into the advantages of personal freedoms in the U.S. Significantly expanded funding would allow the centers to expand their library holdings, courses, and programs.
- Exchange and training programs for leaders of democratic institutions. The International Visitors Program of USIA and AFL/CIO's George Meany Institute are both examples of ef-

fective programs that bring leaders from Central America, as well as from other regions, to the United States for training programs. Additional programs should be established to bring leaders of such democratic institutions as labor unions, local governments, legislatures, and professional associations to work and study in counterpart U.S. organizations.

We also recommend a number of other policies and programs for the U.S. public and private sectors in the areas of trade, investment, and agriculture. These, too, are important elements of a broad-based effort to help the Central American countries prosper, and we now turn to them.

Expanded Trade Opportunities

Rapid Central American economic growth requires increased foreign exchange earnings. In the short run the region will continue to rely largely on the earnings which come from the export of commodities. The Commission considered, and rejected as ineffective or inappropriate, proposals to stabilize commodity prices or earnings. Thus, until demand recovers for the commodities which Central America produces, the prospects for significant increases in export earnings are limited.

The solution to this problem will necessarily be a slow one. Over the medium term, the Central American countries should try to broaden their export bases both in the agricultural and manufactured good sectors. More diversified exports would help to insulate the region from some of the swings in the international economy.

Central American export-promoting policies will come to naught, however, if the rest of the world fails to open its markets. The United States has taken the lead in this respect and the Caribbean Basin Initiative will provide additional encouragement for the development of new export industries.

The Central American countries should also try to free up foreign exchange resources by reducing energy imports. The United States and other donor nations possess relatively inexpensive technology that could be used in the region to identify and explore local energy resources.

We encourage the extension of duty-free trade to Central America by other major trading countries.

The CBI is a landmark piece of legislation and we hope that other countries will be willing to extend similar benefits to Central America. We urge the European Community to extend trade preferences to Central America under the Lome Agreement, since the U.S. is extending CBI benefits to Lome beneficiaries in the Caribbean. Other countries of Latin America should also be encouraged to offer special trade benefits to the Central American countries as their own economic recovery progresses.

We urge the United States to review non-tariff barriers to imports from Central America.

We recognize that this issue—which principally applies to products like textiles, sugar, and meat—is highly contentious, both internationally and domestically. All of these products are affected by multilateral agreements which partly determine the degree of access to the United States market. We encourage the President to use whatever flexibility exists in such agreements in favor of Central American producers.

We recommend technical and financial support for export promotion efforts.

U.S. economic assistance should be used to provide technical and financial support for trading and export marketing companies and innovative export-oriented joint ventures between Central American and foreign entrepreneurs. This is already an important element of the current assistance program; in the future this should be a top priority.

Improved Investment Conditions

The Central American countries must improve the climate for both domestic and foreign investment. These countries could eventually become important production centers for low- and medium-technology goods to be exported to the United States, the rest of Latin America, and Europe. Panamanian leaders already are studying the experiences of Hong Kong, Singapore, and others in an effort to imitate their success as leading producers for export. In addition, increased investment should be encouraged in industries which produce for local consumption.

Of course, peace is necessary before businesses will look seriously at new investment prospects. Without peace, capital flight will continue (although improved financial policies seem to have considerably reduced the outflows), infrastructure will be destroyed, credit will remain unavailable, and private sector initiative will be discouraged. But these countries also need to move now on changing those economic policies that discourage investment.

Several initiatives could be undertaken by the United States to encourage U.S. investors to consider projects in Central America.

We encourage the formation of a privately owned venture capital company for Central America.

We recommend that a venture capital company—which might be called the Central American Development Corporation (CADC)—be established for Central America. This was suggested to us by several private businessmen and organizations and represents an innovative way to promote investment in the region even under present difficult conditions. CADC, capitalized by private sector investors, would use its capital to raise funds which, in turn, would be lent to private companies active in Central America. It would be managed and directed by experienced entrepreneurs. Its loans would be made to commercially viable projects in high priority economic sectors for working capital or investment purposes. The U.S. government could support the CADC initiative through a long-term loan as it has for similar initiatives in other areas of the world.

The United States is about to join the Inter-American Investment Corporation, which has been formed within the Inter-American Development Bank. This new multilateral organization will provide technical support, equity, and loans to private sector companies which are active in the region. This is a potentially useful initiative and we hope that the Congress responds favorably to authorizing legislation when it is submitted later this year.

We recommend the expanded availability of OPIC insurance in the region.

Needed foreign investment could be encouraged through an expanded insurance guarantee program. The Overseas Private Investment Corporation continues to consider investment applications, but because of current political conditions it extends insurance in very few instances. Leading private businessmen told the Commission that the unavailability of such insurance is an obstacle to investment in projects that otherwise have good prospects for commercial success. OPIC should have the resources and the mandate to provide such support.

We recommend the development of aid programs to nurture small businesses, including microbusinesses.

The small business forms the backbone of these economies. Economic aid programs specifically aimed at encouraging the growth and formation of such businesses would assist in putting more people to work and also give people a larger stake in their economies. Such programs should include such incentives as seed capital, loan guarantees, and technical assistance.

Accelerated Agricultural Development

Central America's rural areas contain the majority of the region's poor. They also have the greatest potential for rapid increases in production, particularly in the historically neglected sector which produces food for local consumption rather than for export.

Integrated programs of rural development targeted at the food-producing sector have enormous potential for improving the welfare of large numbers of people, while increasing and diversifying agricultural production and lessening dependence on food imports. Such programs require a variety of coordinated measures which would have to be undertaken by the Central Americans themselves, either by the governments of the region or by regional institutions. They should:

• Provide long-term credit at positive but moderate real interest rates to make possible the purchase of land by small farmers.

[68]

- Study the holding of idle but potentially productive land, and programs to capture capital gains from public works for the public.
- Improve title registration and the defense of property rights of farmers.
- Provide short- and medium-term credit to finance the harvesting and storage of crops, the purchase of fertilizers and other inputs, and the acquisition of machinery and equipment.
- Follow pricing policies for agricultural commodities that protect farmers against unnecessary price fluctuations and unfair marketing practices, that avoid a "cheap food" policy which favors urban consumers and acts as a disincentive to producers, and that discourage the accumulation of unmarketable surpluses.
- Where appropriate, initiate programs of agrarian reform—of "land for the landless"—in order to distribute more equitably the agricultural wealth of the country.
- Expand the network of rural feeder roads, storage facilities, and rural electrification.
- Sharply increase rural research and extension services specifically targeted to crops produced for the domestic market.
- Clarify the legal status and use of public lands, to check deforestation and the degradation of the environment.

These measures involve staggering administrative requirements for governments committed to creating a diversified rural economy in which medium and small private farmers will predominate. That commitment, the political will, and most of the administrative skills cannot be provided by foreigners. Where the commitment exists, however, external help from multilateral institutions and from the United States and other countries could make a crucial contribution.

In particular:

We recommend that the financial underpinnings of the efforts to broaden land ownership be strengthened and reformed.

We have argued that more equitable distribution of income and wealth, including land holdings, is important to economic, social, and political development in the region. In programs of

[69]

land reform, ways should be found to ensure that the redistribution of land provides the new owners with a valid title, that governments promptly allocate resources as they become available to ensure that former owners are effectively compensated, and that in the end the system enhances incentives to expand the nation's total agricultural output.

We recommend the provision of financial resources to supplement credit and investment programs.

A key thrust of U.S. bilateral assistance should be to supplement national and regional agriculture credit programs; this is an element of AID's program which should be expanded in the future. In addition, the program of seasonal agricultural credit both for imported inputs and working capital which was included in the emergency stabilization program should be regularized and expanded in the medium term.

We recommend increased economic support for cooperatives.

Agricultural cooperatives have been important in both U.S. and Central American rural development. They not only encourage increased production through the pooling of resources and sharing of risk, but contribute to improved distribution of income. We recommend that the United States increase its support for such organizations as part of its bilateral aid program.

ORGANIZING FOR DEVELOPMENT

Our second major area of recommendations involves the structure and form of the development effort. The proposals we put forward in this chapter and the next are not a final blueprint for economic and social development. This Commission is acutely aware of its own limitations. We cannot provide what is most vitally needed: a positive Central American vision of the future, and a process for translating that vision into reality. This can only be done by engaging the initiative, the energy and the dedication of the Central Americans themselves, in cooperation with their allies, in a forum capable of addressing the development of the region in all its dimensions, on a continuing basis.

We received many suggestions on how to structure such a process. It was clear from these proposals, and from our own deliberations, that what is required is not another institution competitive with AID, the Inter-American Development Bank or the International Monetary Fund. Nor should such an international organization supersede local development bodies and initiatives. Responsibility for the modernization of each country must lie with its own public and private institutions. Rather, we propose the establishment of a structure which would do what no existing national or international body now does: provide a continuous and coherent approach to the development of the region, a process of review of that development, and access to that process by those who have not before been an integral part of it.

What follows is our distillation of many different proposals. We hope that it will attract the interest of leaders, private and public, within Central America. We are fully aware that no development organization for Central America will have any more consequence than the people of Central America are prepared to give it; any institution must represent the initiative and enjoy the support of the nations of the region or it cannot succeed, however great the enthusiasm for it in Washington.

What will be required, therefore, is a serious examination here and in Central America of how the essential cooperation among nations for development can be achieved and institutionalized. As we suggested earlier, the leaders of Central America and of the United States should then meet to define, together, the opportunity for comprehensive regional development, the principles which should underlie it, and the ways of giving organizational form and process to that common aspiration.

From our own consideration of that issue we have distilled the following principles, which we recommend for consideration:

• The development of Central America should be a cooperative program. The policy issues involved should be addressed through a process of joint deliberation among the nations of Central America, the United States, and such other democracies as may be willing to participate and to provide assistance.

• The program should promote the development of Central America in all its dimensions—economic prosperity, social change, political modernization and peace. Past development efforts have focused too exclusively on economic issues and programs. External aid should be tied to measurable progress toward all of these agreed goals.

• The assessment of progress should be conducted by representatives of participating nations who have access to a broad range of information and experience from both public and private sources. Private groups and institutions in donor and recipient countries should be drawn fully into the deliberative process.

• The ultimate control of aid funds will always rest with the donors. But a multilateral body including eminent Central Americans can most effectively—and least offensively—assess progress, evaluate program objectives, and measure external resource needs. In addition, the multilateral body should exercise some degree of control over development funds to give its assessments added weight, even though donors would retain a veto.

• The structure must be established on a sufficiently permanent basis to demonstrate the long-term commitment of both the United States and the Central American countries to the coordination of economic development with social and political development. The continued utility of the organization should be assessed after five years.

These principles could be served through a variety of organizational structures. We have developed the outline of a structure which we have called the Central American Development Organization, or CADO. We put it forward not as the only design, but as a means of illustrating how the concept could be implemented.

Membership in CADO, as we envision it, would initially be open to the seven countries of Central America—Belize, Costa Rica, El Salvador, Guatemala, Honduras, Nicaragua and Panama —and to the United States. Associate member status would be available to any democracy willing to contribute significant resources to promote regional development. We would hope that the other Contadora countries would participate actively, as well as the nations of Europe, Canada and Japan. The organization's

Chairman should be from the United States with an Executive Secretary from Central America.

The operating body of CADO, in which each full member would be represented, would assess the progress made by each Central American country toward economic, political and social objectives, as well as make recommendations on the allocation of economic resources. It would require of its members a high degree of integrity and judgment; they would be expected to bring to their tasks special competence and experience in the development process. We are convinced that the region has an impressive store of men and women, dedicated to the future progress of their people, who could fill these roles.

Representation should be drawn primarily from the private sector. Each country delegation should include representatives of a democratic trade union movement, of business and/or the government. It would draw on a wide variety of sources for information and for economic, political and human rights analysis including, for example, the deliberations of the Economic Consultative Group, now being organized by the IDB; AID; advisory opinions from the Inter-American Court of Human Rights; the ILO; the Inter-American Human Rights Commission of the Organization of American States; and national monitoring bodies and appropriate private parties.

Central American participation in the program should turn on acceptance of and continued progress toward:

• The protection of personal and economic liberties, freedom of expression, respect for human rights, and an independent system of equal justice and criminal law enforcement.

• Political pluralism, and a process of recurrent elections with competing political parties. Only nations prepared to base their governments on the free choice of their people should be eligible. This does not necessarily mean that each country would institutionalize its political processes in the same way as the United States, but it does mean that each would adopt democratic forms appropriate to its own conditions.

• As set out more fully in Chapter 7, a commitment to preserve peace, independence and the mutual security of Central American member nations by renouncing intervention and limiting arms, as expressed in the reciprocal exchange of mutual security undertakings.

• The establishment and maintenance of sound growth policies in the various countries, including tax and land reforms, and the invigoration of community trade and monetary programs.

• The development of the human resources of the region, as set forth in Chapter 5.

This commitment would be embodied in a charter. CADO would be inaugurated at a summit of the participating countries, at which the charter would be signed.

Nicaragua would be encouraged to participate in CADO in the interest of promoting authentic political pluralism and economic and social development in that country in harmony with the rest of the region. However, Nicaragua's—or any other country's—continued membership in CADO and access to aid within the CADO framework would be conditioned on continued progress toward defined political, social, and economic goals. If Nicaragua—or any other country—concluded that it was unable in good faith to commit itself to permit elections and guarantee human rights and thus failed to join CADO, it would not, in our judgment, affect the ultimate effectiveness of the organization.

We recommend that an economic reconstruction fund be established within CADO and that the U.S. channel one-quarter of its economic assistance through such a fund. Loans to countries would be in support of development programs and policies including the implementation of growth-oriented economic policies, the establishment of genuine democratic institutions, and the adoption of programs to improve social conditions. They would be quick-disbursing, balance of payments support loans.

Our overall objective in putting forward these institutional proposals is substantive, not structural. The crisis in Central America is region-wide; it cannot be resolved piecemeal. It will require local effort and external support, integrated into a comprehensive approach on security, economic, political and social needs. The assessment of that effort should be multilateral as well.

One historic model for this proposal is the Inter-American

Committee for the Alliance for Progress, or CIAP from its Spanish-language acronym. This was a distinguished group of persons from the hemisphere, including one U.S. representative. They regularly reviewed and provided independent commentary on the national economic policies and programs of the Alliance members. Since they were mostly Latin Americans and seen to be unbiased, their advice was accepted in the constructive spirit in which it was given. We have been told by former members of CIAP and former officials who figured in the Alliance for Progress effort that a similar arrangement for Central America would make a valuable contribution.

Governments, including that of the United States, would not be bound to accept the judgments of CADO. The U.S. would be free to maintain a bilateral economic assistance program in a particular country, regardless of performance. But the present purely bilateral process has its drawbacks. It factors political assessments directly into economic aid decisions. This makes the United States the prosecutor, judge and jury. It leads to rancorous debate, sometimes poorly informed. This Commission's proposal is an effort to explore a new process. The responsibility for assessing development performance would be assumed in the first instance by a respected multilateral body, with donors retaining effective final control of their financial resources. The process should be more effective, more acceptable to Central America and more compatible with present-day views of how sovereign nations should deal with each other.

Appendix to Chapter 4

CENTRAL AMERICAN FINANCIAL NEEDS

Forecasts of Central America's net foreign financial needs (which are defined as the sum of a country's balance of payments current account deficit plus minimal foreign reserve build-up) depend on a number of factors including the countries' economic policies, the political climate in the region, the ability of national and regional institutions to use increased assistance productively, and the international economic and financial environment. The financial requirements also depend on the economic goal: the more rapidly these economies grow, the greater their financial need. Faster growth—at least in Central America—would both require and lead to higher levels of imports; if export earnings do not grow as rapidly, then the resulting increase in the deficit must be financed by grants, loans, or investments.

The ultimate economic goal of an expanded financial assistance program should be to help the Central American countries re-create the conditions necessary for sustainable economic growth. In practical terms, the program should focus on helping these countries at least to reachieve 1980 levels of per capita income by the end of this decade. Because of the depth and duration of the economic decline throughout Central America over the past several years, returning to 1980 levels will be difficult, attainable only with an enormous, sustained effort by both the Central Americans and their bilateral and multilateral creditors. Average real growth of about 6 percent annually (or 3 percent on a per capita basis) is an ambitious but realistic target by the end of the decade; this would be sufficient to absorb new entrants to the labor market and to reduce unemployment.

There are four key sets of assumptions that underlie our estimates of medium-term financial needs:

• PEACE. Without a considerable reduction in the levels of violence, efforts to revive the regional economy will fail. Economic and financial incentives to invest or even to produce would be overwhelmed by the direct and indirect effects of political turmoil. Capital flight would continue, draining the new financial resources which we propose be made available. Moreover, the continuing destruction of infrastructure in El Salvador would raise further the cost of economic reconstruction in that country.

• IMPROVED ECONOMIC POLICY. We assume that, over time, the Central American countries will considerably improve their economic performance. Public sector deficits must be controlled through appropriate fiscal policies. Public investment programs should be reoriented towards maintenance and rehabilitation. A growing share of public sector capital expenditures should be diverted to providing credit to the private sector, in order to alleviate the difficult financial conditions of many firms. Export taxes and other export disincentives should be reduced or eliminated, and each of these countries should maintain a realistic exchange rate policy. In addition, local banking systems need to be made more efficient, and appropriate incentives to encourage savings and investment should be provided.

• INCREASED ECONOMIC ASSISTANCE. We assume that considerably increased economic assistance will be made available from bilateral and multilateral sources starting in 1984. If this assistance is delayed, economic recovery will also lag and the 1990 target will be even more difficult to achieve.

• IMPROVED GLOBAL ECONOMIC ENVIRONMENT. We assume that international economic and financial conditions will continue to improve. Relatively strong growth, stable or declining interest rates, and low inflation in the major developed countries are critical to the health of the Central American economies. These conditions would result in improved demand for manufactured goods and commodity exports. If export market access improves and if increased investment leads to greater manufactured export capacity, the region's export revenues could increase, despite the poor price outlook for Central America's key commodity exports. The region's terms of trade—the ratio of export prices to import prices—have fallen more than 60 percent in the last five years and only modest recovery is expected.

Macroeconomic projections have been prepared for Costa Rica, El Salvador, Guatemala, Honduras, Nicaragua, and Panama through 1990. The combination of peace, much improved economic performance, increased foreign assistance, higher export demand, and improved market access would allow these countries to find a way out of the crisis. Export income would increase and imports could follow. Overall per capita growth, and more particularly consumption, could at least regain the levels of 1980 and, in some cases, the late 1970's. Unemployment would begin falling.

In aggregate, the six countries would have a cumulative net financing requirement of around $24 billion. Excluding Nicaragua

—which is the only one of these countries which today does not receive U.S. economic assistance—the total would be almost $21 billion.

External Financing Requirements, 1984–1990*

Costa Rica	$ 5.1
El Salvador	5.5
Guatemala	4.5
Honduras	2.3
Panama	3.2
Subtotal	20.6
Nicaragua	3.4
TOTAL	$24.0

*Projected aggregate net financing requirements associated with achieving 1980 per capita GDP levels in 1990. For Panama the goal is to maintain 1982 per capita GNP, since through last year the economy continued to expand.

These projections may underestimate the region's financing needs by assuming that capital flight is eliminated after 1983, commercial and financial arrears are fully capitalized, maturing public and private debts are refinanced, and most important, the bulk of new financial resources goes to investment rather than consumption. None of these assumptions is likely to be realized fully; the overall *net* borrowing requirement would inevitably be greater. In addition, the *gross* financing requirement would be larger by the amount of scheduled amortization, which is estimated at about $5 billion. These debts will have to be restructured, which is a burden on the creditors, but does not represent a new transfer of financial resources.

This enormous financing requirement reflects the extremely adverse economic developments of the past years, the structural weaknesses of the Central American economies, the need to rebuild infrastructure in El Salvador and Nicaragua, and the likelihood that even steady progress to develop export capacity through appropriate incentives and accelerated investment will only gradually have a significant impact on export revenues. At the same time, these funds will not stimulate the projected economic recovery unless the Central American countries make a determined effort to restructure their economies.

The bulk of the projected financing needs would have to be met by official creditors. Over the next several years commercial banks are likely to be reluctant to increase their exposure in Central America. However, some $4 billion of interest payments to banks are due during 1984–1990. Based on the refinancing proposals which are being discussed or are in place, it seems reasonable to assume that at least half of these amounts will be reloaned. This fraction could rise as economic performance improves. In addition, several of the countries are likely to attract some private investment flows, especially in the context of an improving political and economic environment. In total these private sources could provide as much as $6 billion of new loans or investments. Thus, official sources would probably have to provide around $18 billion.

For the U.S. this would mean at least $10 to $12 billion over the seven years, assuming that World Bank, Inter-American Development Bank, and other bilateral creditors such as Mexico and Venezuela increase their assistance programs at least modestly from current levels. A successful effort to increase assistance from these organizations or to encourage European and Japanese participation would reduce the share needed from the United States.

In the short run, the financing needs in 1984 of the six countries which now receive U.S. economic assistance are estimated to be around $1.5 to $1.7 billion, based on forecasts of their export earnings and internal economic activity. The uncovered gap—after identified lending and investment including budgeted U.S. economic assistance—seems to be as much as $0.6 billion. Thus, we have recommended an emergency increase in U.S. economic assitance to help cover this shortfall, so that the near-term prospects of economic recovery will not dim further.

One adverse consequence of an ambitious recovery and reconstruction program would be a sharp increase in debt levels in all the Central American countries unless the terms on which new assistance is extended are highly concessional. Such an increased debt burden would permanently mortgage Central America's future, almost regardless of efforts to enhance export (and, hence, debt service) capacity.

CHAPTER 5

HUMAN DEVELOPMENT

A COMPREHENSIVE EFFORT to promote democracy and prosperity among the Central American nations must have as its cornerstone accelerated "human development." Widespread hunger and malnutrition, illiteracy, poor educational and training opportunities, poor health conditions, and inadequate housing are unstable foundations on which to encourage the growth of viable democratic institutions.

In this chapter we focus on social conditions, and on efforts which can be undertaken in both the short and medium term to help Central Americans improve their living conditions. The burden of action in these areas, even more than in some others, lies primarily on the Central Americans themselves. However well-intentioned, no foreigner can feed, educate, doctor, clothe and house another country's people without undermining its government or creating cultural conflicts. However, the United States can provide some of the resources which the Central Americans need to make their programs work, and it can counsel on the design of those programs.

Many Central Americans with whom we met emphasized the importance of bold initiatives to improve Central American living conditions. In this spirit, we believe the following are ambitious yet realistic objectives for the 1980's:

- The reduction of malnutrition.
- The elimination of illiteracy.
- Universal access to primary education.
- Universal access to primary health care.
- A significant reduction of infant mortality.
- A sustained reduction in population growth rates.
- A significant improvement in housing.

The programs we outline below are intended to help Central Americans achieve these objectives. Such funds as they require from the U.S. government would be part of the expanded economic assistance program described in the previous chapter.

Developing Educational Opportunites

Central American countries suffer from widespread illiteracy, from insufficient numbers and inadequate quality of primary and secondary schools, and from shortages of vocational training opportunities. Adult literacy is lowest in Guatemala (45% of the population in 1976), Honduras (60% in 1980), and El Salvador (63%). Nicaragua now claims 90% literacy. Costa Rica (90%), Panama (85%) and Belize (92%) all have high literacy rates, although there are sharp differences between urban and rural rates. For example, in Panama rural literacy is only 65% compared to 94% in the urban areas.

Although over the past twenty years there have been improvements in the system, educational quality continues to be generally poor. Educational content often has little relevance to the practical needs of students, and there is a mismatch in all countries between needed skills and the supply of persons trained in those skills. Poorly trained and motivated teachers, as well as inadequate physical facilities, textbooks, teacher's guides, basic educational materials and supplies are pervasive problems.

In general, the Central American educational system is weakest at its base: the quality of primary education is low, and dropout rates are high, despite laws mandating universal compulsory primary education throughout the region. The problems are particularly acute in rural areas where only three or four years of education are the norm. Only a portion of students—under 40% in Honduras, Guatemala, El Salvador and Nicaragua (1975 statistics)—is retained through the primary level.

The problems of the primary education system extend through the secondary, vocational and higher education systems. Less than 50% of the eligible population is enrolled at the secondary level in most countries of the region. Schools are overcrowded, teacher salaries are low, and many teachers are ill-prepared. Similarly, vocational training opportunities are relatively limited, underfunded, and not well matched to critical skill shortages. Universities suffer from overextended facilities, overemphasis on traditional fields (such as the law) at the expense of applied disciplines (such as business, management, the natural sciences, engineering, and agriculture), poorly trained instructors, and extremely high attrition rates. Moreover, many of the universities have become highly politicized, more concerned with political activism than with educating students to meet the concrete needs of their countries.

We agree with the many Central Americans who told us that a substantial improvement in the availability and quality of educational opportunities must begin at once and proceed as rapidly as possible. The nations of Central America clearly understand the importance of education and have made a commitment to it. Although Central American initiatives and organizations must carry the burden of designing educational programs and reforms, there is also a great need for financial and technical assistance for educational reforms and training programs. This assistance can be provided by the United States, multilateral organizations, and other countries.

Educational advance also, very centrally, requires solving a key health problem: malnutrition. If children are malnourished in their earliest years, they come to school mentally and physically underdeveloped and the learning process is almost inevitably set back. In testimony before the Commission, Dr. Nevin Scrimshaw, founder of Nutrition Institute for Central America and Panama, brought the dismaying message that malnutrition in Central America, after modest reductions, has returned to the levels of the 1950's. In El Salvador, 73 percent of the schoolchildren now suffer from malnutrition. Dr. Frank Marasciulo, Executive Vice President of the Pan American Development Foundation, reported to the Commission that 52 percent of the people in the region are malnourished.

The Commission concludes that the first priority for education in Central America should be nutritional programs sufficient to deliver children to school in normal physical and mental condition.

We recommend that the United States increase food aid on an emergency basis.

Although the permanent solution to the problem lies in accelerated agricultural development, the United States and other donors—including members of the European Community—can help in the short run by providing additional food aid. The United States now provides about $100 million annually to Central America in such aid through the PL 480 program. This should be expanded, and also supplemented by increased use of the Commodity Credit Corporation program in Central America. In addition, the food distribution system needs to be improved to absorb increased levels of assistance effectively.

The United States and other countries can help Central Americans improve educational training opportunities. This should focus principally on building institutions, although in the short run direct training programs may be needed while institutions develop. The effort should start with a literacy program and continue with programs to help improve the quality and broaden the availability of formal education and vocational training programs.

We recommend that the Peace Corps expand its recruitment of front line teachers to serve in a new Literacy Corps.

A Literacy Corps of qualified volunteeers should be created to engage in direct teaching and also to train Central Americans to teach their compatriots. The Peace Corps has had long experience in this function. We urge a dramatic expansion of volunteers in the region from the current 600 to a figure five or six times as great, largely in education. Emphasis in recruitment should be on mature persons who speak Spanish. Other democratic countries in Latin America should be encouraged to offer similar groups of volunteers to help combat illiteracy.

The Literacy Corps would be a remedial effort for adults and children over ten who received no schooling at all. To ensure that remedial programs in literacy will not be needed beyond 1990, primary education must be made available to all children.

We recommend that Peace Corps activities be expanded at the primary, secondary, and technical levels in part by establish-

ing a Central American Teacher Corps, recruited from the Spanish-speaking population of the United States.

Here again, we believe that other democracies in Latin America should be encouraged to undertake similar programs, and that the countries themselves should dramatize the education effort by seeking local volunteers.

The primary schools are the proper focus for a wide range of social programs. Basic public health, including nutrition, is much easier to assure when a teacher monitors the condition of pupils on a day-to-day basis. Inoculations can be given cheaply and effectively as part of the school's routine.

We recommend an expanded program of secondary level technical and vocational education.

Although both the public and private sectors are already active in this area, there is a substantial need for additional training programs matched to real jobs. We particularly urge that business and labor unions develop apprenticeship programs.

Vocational training is particularly needed in agriculture, which is the mainstay of the Central American economies. Drawing on its own agricultural experience, the United States can offer increased technical support to help Central Americans improve production and productivity of both cash and food crops. The United States should also provide both technical support and financial assistance to national agricultural centers. These centers can provide valuable training and technical assistance to farmers and can form the core of national and regional agricultural extension efforts.

Business and public administration are also crucial to the future development of the region. Existing institutions such as the Central American Institute for Business Administration (INCAE) could benefit from increased support from both public and private sector sources.

We recommend expansion of the International Executive Service Corps (IESC).

The IESC is a private, voluntary organization of retired American business executives. An expanded IESC effort in Central America, perhaps with some support from the U.S. Government, should give particular attention to training managers of small businesses. This would strengthen the economy, while also contributing to the development of the middle class.

A major shortcoming of past U.S. educational assistance has been insufficient support for Central American universities and university students. By contrast, higher education is increasingly a major focus of the efforts of the Soviet Union and Cuba in the region. According to USIA, total Soviet, Eastern European, and Cuban university scholarships to Central Americans reached 7,500 in 1982, representing a seven-fold increase over the last five years. By comparison, in 1982 only 391 Central American students were supported in this country by U.S. government sponsored scholarships. Overall Central American enrollment in U.S. universities was around 7,200. Nevertheless, such educational opportunities in the United States are generally limited to students from families with relatively high incomes. The targeting of students from lower income families and the large number of government scholarships distinguish Cuban and Soviet educational strategy from that of the United States.

In all the Central American countries, political and academic leaders emphasized the long-run cost of having so many of Central America's potential future leaders—especially those from disadvantaged backgrounds—educated in Soviet Bloc countries. We agree that a major initiative is needed and should be an essential part of a comprehensive development effort.

Thus, we recommend a program of 10,000 government-sponsored scholarships to bring Central American students to the United States.

The United States should provide 5,000 four- to six-year university scholarships and 5,000 two- to four-year vocational-technical scholarships. Admittedly, this is an ambitious program compared both to current efforts and to the 500 scholarships anticipated under the CBI. Nevertheless, it is imperative to offer young Central Americans the opportunity to study in the United States, both to improve the range and quality of educational alternatives and to build lasting links between Central America and the United States.

We suggest that such a program involve the following elements:

- Careful targeting to encourage participation by young people from all social and economic classes.
- Maintenance of existing admission standards—which has sometimes been a barrier in the past—by providing intensive English and other training as part of the program.
- Mechanisms to encourage graduates to return to their home countries after completing their education, perhaps by providing part of the educational support in the form of loans and linking forgiveness of loans to their return.
- Arrangements by which the Central American countries bear some of the cost of the program.
- The availability of at least 100 to 200 of these scholarships to mid-career public service officials and a further 100 for University faculty exchanges.

We are aware that such a program may be viewed as too expensive and too dramatic. Experts have testified to the Commission that once in place, such a large-scale program would cost about $100 million. Because of the important implications which the training of a country's future leaders has on its political development, we believe this would represent a sound investment of U.S. assistance funds. We hope that such a program would be supplemented by significant private sector efforts. U.S. universities, faced with declining enrollments, will have hundreds of thousands of places by 1990 and could readily accommodate these students in existing programs. The universities would themselves benefit from attracting additional Central American students to their campuses.

We recommend that the United States, in close partnership with the Central American governments and universities, develop a long-term plan to strengthen the major universities in Central America.

The principal thrust of this assistance effort should be to help improve the quality of Central American universities. A balanced program of assistance would include:

- Technical assistance to provide immediate improvements in undergraduate teaching and curriculum.
- Selective investments in improving libraries, laboratories, and student facilities.
- An innovative effort to recruit and train junior faculty and young administrators.
- A complementary program of refresher training and upgrading of existing faculty and administrative staff.
- An expanded program of pairing of U.S. and Central American colleges and universities.
- A significant expansion of opportunities for faculty, students, and administrators to visit the United States for periods which may range from a few weeks to several years.

We recommend that the United States help strengthen Central American judicial systems.

In the absence of strong legal institutions, political, security and economic crises are magnified. This has been particularly true in El Salvador, where the virtual collapse of the nation's criminal justice system both reflects and exacerbates the inability of the government to control the prevailing cycle of violence and intimidation. In other Central American countries, notably Costa Rica and Honduras, the legal systems are not in a similar state of crisis. Nevertheless, the long-term vitality of these crucial legal institutions could benefit substantially from U.S. assistance to indigenous efforts to strengthen them and to advance the rule of law, in particular by improving the training of judges and investigators.

Specifically, we recommend the use of U.S. economic assistance to:

- Enhance the training and resources of judges, judicial staff, and public prosecutors' offices.
- Support modern and professional means of criminal investigation.
- Promote availability of legal materials, assistance to law faculties, and support for local bar associations.

U.S. assistance policy has failed in the past to reflect the importance of such steps. We recommend that recent U.S. efforts to begin a program of support for legal institutions be formalized, expanded, and expressly funded. Much of this training would be best supplied by U.S. universities with appropriate legal and criminal justice programs.

Other cultural and educational activities should also be encouraged. We should seek particularly to bridge the gap between U.S. and Latin American cultures. For instance, a book translation and distribution program sponsored by the U.S. Information Agency which was once extensive but has lately been withering away should be given support. Translation in both directions is currently limited in scope and often in quality.

We recommend a greatly expanded effort, subsidized by the U.S. Government through the National Endowment for the Humanities, to train high-level translators, to support translations of important books from both languages, and to subsidize their publication so as to make them generally available.

The National Endowment could make an important contribution to U.S.-Central American understanding through such a center.

A REGION'S HEALTH

If Disraeli's view that the "economic health of a nation depends first on the health of its people" is true, then it is vital that health conditions in Central America be improved as a precondition for economic recovery.

The Central American people suffer from extremely poor health conditions, although there are sharp differences among countries. The incidence of infectious diseases, parasitism, malnutrition, tuberculosis and infant mortality has remained virtually unchanged for the last decade. The resurgence of malaria and dengue fever alone will, unchecked, undo any hope of social or economic development. Respiratory illness, diarrheal diseases, and infectious and parasitic diseases that are controlled or cured in developed countries are often fatal in Central America. As

[89]

discussed earlier in this chapter, widespread malnutrition erodes the basis of health care as well as of education.

These conditions affect infants and children with particular severity. Although significant improvements have been achieved over the past two decades, mortality rates for infants and children are substantially higher in Central America than in the rest of Latin America. Infant mortality is higher in Nicaragua (88 per 1000 births in 1980 according to the World Bank), Honduras (86/1000), El Salvador (75/1000) and Guatemala (66/1000). In Belize (30/1000), Costa Rica (27/1000) and Panama (21/1000), mortality rates are lower, reflecting the considerably higher quality of their health care systems.

In nations where swamps provide breeding grounds for mosquitos, where water is neither adequately available nor potable, and where there is limited sewage disposal and poor sanitation, the incidence of many diseases will reach epidemic proportions. Moreover, where medical facilities are few and medical personnel lacking, the possibilities for prevention and cure are restricted.

Considerable effort has been made by the governments of Central America in the support of primary health care, environmental sanitation and population control. There has also been substantial investment of resources in the institutional treatment of disease. Just as in our own country, hospitals are highly visible and their construction is responsive to the demands of the local medical profession. This is a necessary component of any health system, albeit the most expensive form of care. The stress on primary care by international agencies has had the effect of diverting local funding into the tertiary care facilities. The relative lack of concern by such agencies with the funding of health manpower training has also left the Central American countries unable to staff their existing facilities adequately. The low priority given to helping these nations improve their ability to deliver a higher level of health care has been a serious deficiency in development assistance programs.

The United States can play an important role in supporting Central American efforts to achieve adequate and comprehensive health care. The immediate priorities of such a program are the eradication of malnutrition, the provision of primary health care, the prevention of disease, the improvement of health care delivery systems, the development of adequate secondary and tertiary back-up institutions (improving those that already exist—building anew only when essential) and the training of health manpower.

A comprehensive program of primary health care includes both preventive and curative medicine. Secondary and tertiary care should be concentrated in regional centers and hospitals. Improved communication and transportation facilities are essential for the primary health care component which these regional centers will support.

Management and planning for the effective use of scarce resources are at the heart of improving curative and preventive health services.

In order to meet this need, we recommend that existing technical assistance programs supported by AID should be expanded.

Broader concentration should be placed upon health care systems, management health care planning and health economics. These specialities are interrelated; therefore, the training of Central American candidates for them should be carried out in an integrated manner. A regional center for such training should be considered in either Costa Rica or Panama, since both of these nations have comparatively advanced health care and institutional systems.

The present system of health care in Central America rests on a form of government-provided medical service very different from our own. We should not seek to impose our system on those countries, but should seek to expand upon and improve the structures already in place. Central America must develop a system of health care suitable to its own needs. But from our own experience we can advise them that what is needed is not service alone—more doctors, better hospitals or research, important as these are—but the development and expansion of alternative systems of health care delivery and an expanding effort in preventive medicine.

Voluntary private organizations must play a significant role. They have the advantage of being clearly uninvolved in political issues, and they can more readily gain local confidence. U.S. government participation should be limited primarily to providing financing mechanisms to support technical assistance in such key areas as management and planning as well as in the evaluation process. Administration of such funding, as carried out by the American Schools and Hospitals Abroad (ASHA)—the section of AID which supports such institutions—is a good example of public/private cooperation.

The United States government and other donors have already expended considerable resources to promote the development and expansion of health resources in Central America. Since the mid-1970's the major thrust of United States government support has been the extension of primary health care services in rural areas and the development of village-level water systems. These have been important efforts and have contributed to a growing awarenesss that the emphasis of health care services in the region must switch from the costly hospital-based central system to an emphasis on the provision of primary health care. We endorse this approach and urge its expansion, using a portion of the increased economic assistance which we have recommended be made available.

In addition, other measures are needed:

We recommend a resumption of the AID-sponsored program to eradicate vector-borne diseases such as malaria and dengue fever.

An AID-sponsored vector control program was suspended five years ago. However, Belize, Guatemala, Honduras and El Salvador are currently experiencing a serious resurgence of malaria and dengue fever. The mosquito knows no frontiers and Nicaragua, Costa Rica and Panama will soon suffer equally unless drastic measures are taken to eradicate the breeding grounds of the mosquito. Nearly a century ago, malaria and yellow fever were eradicated from areas where they had long held sway. We cannot allow a terrible regression to the past.

Research must be supported so as to find insecticides to which the vectors are not resistant. In the short term we can expand the present programs of spraying with the still-effective insecticides. We should encourage and support engineering projects which would improve drainage and sewage disposal. Additional professionals and volunteers to combat the diseases must be trained.

We recommend that the United States support an expansion of programs of oral rehydration and immunization so as to reduce dramatically the incidence of childhood disease and mortality in Central America during the next five years.

The death rate of children in Central America from diarrheal disease is ten times higher than in the United States. Such other childhood diseases as diphtheria, tetanus, whooping cough, measles and polio remain endemic to the region. Yet the experience of UNICEF, AID and others indicates that these scourges of early childhood can be virtually wiped out in a very short time by well-administered programs of oral rehydration and immunization.

We recommend the continuation of the population and family planning programs currently supported by the Agency for International Development.

Overpopulation presents a serious threat to the development and health of the region. Attempts must be made through education and family planning to reduce the birth rate to a more moderate level.

We recommend that Central American educational institutions be encouraged to increase their concentration on the training of primary health care workers, nurses, dental assistants and personnel in the allied health skills.

The United States, through AID, should provide funds for expanded programs in these areas to be supervised and administered by appropriate divisions of AID, by the Peace Corps, or by private voluntary organizations.

With the exception of Honduras, considerable progress has been made in the training of physicians for local needs, though external training is still required for more sophisticated skills. The training of physicians continues to be a priority; but the training of nurses, dentists and other allied health technicians required for an adequate health system should be increased.

Nursing services are sorely lacking in the region, in part because nursing is not accorded the professional status which it merits. High-quality nursing is an important priority for the region. Thus, we further recommend the establishment of a regional nurses' training unit for the purpose of granting graduate degrees so as to establish a greater pool of indigenous nursing educators. Such a unit could be located in either Panama or Costa Rica.

More village health workers, who live among the people, and who can detect illness, treat minor problems, and provide essential education in health and personal hygiene, the cleanliness of homes and utensils, and nutrition and family planning, must be trained. Training at this level is more cost effective, and has the further advantage that such trainees are more likely to remain in their locales. With proper encouragement and assistance, this training responsibility can be borne by the local professionals.

It is also important to address the general issue of health care reform. At present, governments of the region claim that health care is provided without charge. The unhappy truth is that local facilities are often unable to provide either medication or essential diagnostic services to the poor, because they cannot afford them. Free service is often no service at all. In most of the region, there is also a costly and inefficient duplication of health services between the Ministries of Health and Social Security. Costa Rica has transferred all medical services to a single organization. That pattern should be considered for adoption or adaptation throughout the region.

Many urban centers in Central America now have well-equipped and well-staffed private medical institutions. In considering the development of private sector enterprises, as well as the fulfillment of local needs, a health insurance system could be provided so that these institutions could help bear the load created by the rapidly growing urban populations.

The lessons of experience from Medicare and Medicaid and from private insurance systems in the United States should be brought to bear on the development of demonstration finance systems. Existing social insurance programs should be extended or modified on a country-by-country basis. This is especially significant as the middle class becomes a larger proportion of the population. A fundamental principle should be to ensure equitable medical care for the indigent. This could begin to fill a gap in existing health care systems and avoid the unnecessary duplication of health care programs. It could also provide for a new, local, private sector initiative where none exists, or expand such efforts where they have already begun.

We recommend that the nations of Central America be urged to develop methods which would integrate public and private financing of health services.

In this effort state investment should be focused on primary health care services for the rural and urban poor and on environmental services for all. Specifically, care must be taken to prevent health insurance programs funded in whole or in part from public funds from providing excessive support to hospital services, thereby discouraging adequate public investment in primary care and related preventive and environmental interventions. In every Central American capital city, as well as in many of the larger provincial towns, there are well-equipped private clinics and hospitals available to those who can afford the cost. Health care insurance could be used to make these services more generally available.

Finally, the problems of worker health and safety and industrial pollution must be addressed. Greater attention needs to be paid to standards of worker health and safety. Serious workplace accidents are common. Under present conditions, environmental controls are limited. Uncontrolled waste and indiscriminate use of insecticides and fertilizers are polluting the land, rivers and lakes.

U.S. corporations, active in the region, have a particular responsibility to provide leadership in creating safe and healthy conditions, as well as to introduce appropriate standards of environmental pollution control in their own operations.

HOUSING

Urbanization throughout Central America is rapidly transforming the character of the region. A region-wide movement of peoples, from the countryside to the city, places a strain on all urban facilities. National and local governments are unable to meet the needs of their new residents. Housing and the development of urban services are critical needs, affecting as much as three-quarters of the population, primarily the poor.

Currently over 40% of the region's people live in cities; in Nicaragua and Panama, the majority of the population is urban and, by the turn of the century, all the Central American countries are expected to be predominantly urban. However, the cities lack sufficient resources to cope with their existing populations. The past two decades of growth have outpaced the ability of the institutions and economies of the various nations to provide the whole range of facilities and services we associate with life and work in the modern city—from shelter to basic water and sanitation, electricity and phone service, public transport, garbage collection, fire and ambulance service, etc. Moreover, the economic collapse of the region—which has brought sharply higher levels of unemployment and has further reduced the availability of governmental resources to cope with these problems—has worsened living conditions in the cities even more.

Housing conditions are critical. A very high proportion of dwellings, in both urban and rural areas, are built with non-permanent materials and lack the most elementary sanitary facilities. This is particularly true in El Salvador, Guatemala, Honduras, and Nicaragua. In addition, recent data from these countries show that, on average, almost half of all urban residences lack basic water services and more than 60% lack sewage services. In San Salvador, over one-half the metropolitan area households live in marginal settlements. In 1979 in the metropolitan area of Guatemala City only 44 percent of all households had access to piped water and two-thirds lived in marginal settlements. Conditions in rural areas are worse.

Efforts to improve conditions have fallen far short of the pace of rapidly growing populations; for example, between 1974 and 1978 in Honduras, almost 33,000 new urban households were formed, but only 16,400 new apartments and houses were constructed. Moreover, what construction occurs is primarily for the wealthy. Eighty-six percent of El Salvador's total 1978–79 investment in housing went into dwelling units for households in the top 20 to 25 percent of the income range. In Nicaragua the figure was 88 percent. Similar but less exaggerated trends have existed in other countries of the region.

The prospects for the future are grim. One U.S. government estimate indicates that the number of urban households could increase by more than 4 million between 1985 and the end of the century. Given recent housing construction rates of both private builders and government agencies, less than one-quarter of this need would be met. This inevitably would mean more overcrowding of existing dwellings, further proliferation of marginal and "squatter" settlements, and more pressure on already overburdened services.

Central Americans, in both the public and private sectors, must inevitably bear the major part of the burden of providing adequate shelter to their people. Unfortunately, governmental ineffectiveness and inefficiencies have compounded the problems. Cost recovery is generally not practiced. Subsidies are heavy and not necessarily related to income or wealth. Interest rates are pegged at artificially low levels. Public sector bureaucracies, including city governments, are typically inefficient, overstaffed, and poorly managed. One typical result is that legalization of land tenure has often lagged, without which city services cannot be extended.

The U.S. government and other donors have made housing a priority for many years and have probably prevented an even worse situation from developing. These efforts have included housing guarantee programs, support for the establishment of housing banks and other financial associations, training, technical assistance, and direct financial support for construction financing. These programs should be expanded, in close coordination with the Central Americans, as part of the comprehensive development effort in the region. This also is another area where the private sector, both in the United States and in Central America, can play a valuable role in mobilizing resources and bringing to bear the kinds of practical experience which government organizations often lack.

There are two areas where U.S. assistance should be concentrated.

First, we recommend an enlarged housing and infrastructure construction program.

This recommendation was highlighted in the last chapter, but it is important to stress it again here. AID has estimated that, over the next decade, required housing investment in urban areas will cost some $700 million annually, with another $200 million in related infrastructure costs. Most of this will eventually have to come from local resources, but an expanded aid program could also help. In addition to the benefits from improved housing, construction programs create productive skilled and unskilled jobs. On average, $100 million of additional investment in urban construction annually would support a construction workforce of at least 20,000.

However, it is essential that such a program rely heavily on the private sector for both design and implementation. There is considerable unused capacity in both the U.S. and Central American construction industries that could be harnessed to expand the production of shelter and related infrastructure.

Second, we recommend U.S. government support for accelerated education and training of professionals in public administration.

In our earlier discussion of educational needs and priorities we identified such training as essential in many fields. Improved public sector management—through better-trained managers—is critical to addressing the housing and shelter problems of the region in both the short and medium term. This should occur both through scholarship and exchange programs in the United States and by providing resources to national and regional public administration institutes.

HUMANITARIAN RELIEF

The tragedy of the more than one million displaced persons in Central America—driven from their homes by violence and fear of violence—is well known. Those who have found refuge in Mexico, Honduras and Costa Rica are being adequately cared for under the auspices of the United Nations High Commissioner for Refugees. However, hundreds of thousands remain in El Salvador and Guatemala living under the most miserable conditions. These nations, whose economies have been seriously disrupted, cannot by themselves provide adequate care or relief for these people. The refugee camps and overcrowded cities to which they have fled become breeding grounds for discontent and frustration.

The Commission believes that effective relief efforts which would assist these people would not only serve a humanitarian purpose but would have a positive effect on the political, social and economic future of the countries involved.

We recommend expanded support for adequate relief efforts through the Agency for International Development and the Department of State refugee program.

The Needed Commitment

The recommendations we have made in this chapter constitute an ambitious program of human development in Central America. They cannot be accomplished by appropriations of money alone. Stability and security in the hemisphere depend on the existence of democratic and economically viable nations in Central America. In turn, this requires that their people be healthy, educated, properly housed and free.

To achieve this requires a consensus in the United States that the welfare of Central America is crucial to the well-being of the United States itself, and a commitment by thousands of corporations and individuals—as well as by the government—to help improve living conditions throughout Central America. We believe that if this development effort is to succeed, it must be supported by the educational and business institutions of this country. Such support is clearly in our own best interests, as well as in those of the Central American nations.

CHAPTER 6

CENTRAL AMERICAN SECURITY ISSUES

WE ARDENTLY WISH that there were no need for a security chapter in a report on Central America. But there is.

The region is torn by war and the threat of war. It needs peace in order to have progress. It needs security in order to have peace.

The conflicts that ravage the nations of Central America have both indigenous and foreign roots. Restoring peace and stability will require a combination of social and political reforms, economic advances, diplomatic pursuit and military effort. In earlier chapters we dealt with the social, economic and political aspects; in the next chapter, we will discuss possible diplomatic measures. We hope that negotiations will bear fruit so that the people of Central America can devote their energies to bettering their lives. That is our strong preference—a vigorous, concrete and comprehensive diplomatic effort is set forth in the next section. But even as military measures are needed to shield economic and social programs, so too are they essential as an adjunct to diplomacy.

Thus, in this chapter, we discuss the military and strategic aspects—first in their wider dimensions, and then in terms of the specific situations now confronting us in Central America.

We have stressed before, and we repeat here: indigenous reform movements, even indigenous revolutions, are not themselves a security concern of the United States. History holds examples of genuinely popular revolutions, springing wholly from native roots. In this hemisphere Mexico is a clear example. But during the past two decades we have faced a new phenomenon. The concerting of the power of the Soviet Union and Cuba to extend their presence and influence into vulnerable areas of the Western Hemisphere is a direct threat to U.S. security interests. This type of insurgency is present in Central America today.

The complexity of the political conflicts in Central America aggravates the situation in several countries and sometimes obscures the outlines of the different contests that are under way.

In Somoza's Nicaragua three broad groups were involved in the struggle for decisive control of that country: the Somoza machine, which dominated the country's government, army and economy; oppositionists who desired to establish democratic institutions including free elections and all the associated guarantees; and Marxist-Leninists who were tied to Cuba and the Soviet bloc.

After 1978 those in Nicaragua who opposed the Somoza regime joined together in a single "broad front" which eventually overthrew the Somozas. In the ensuing struggle, the Marxist-Leninist FSLN, with a monopoly of military power, took control of the machinery of government. They have since used that control effectively to exclude the democratic opposition from power. Some of the latter continue their struggle today as leaders of an armed insurgency against the Nicaraguan government.

In El Salvador two separate conflicts have raged since 1979. One conflict pits persons seeking democratic government and its associated rights and freedoms against those trying to maintain oligarchical rule and its associated privileges. A second conflict pits guerrillas seeking to establish a Marxist-Leninist state as part of a broader Central American revolution against those who oppose a Marxist-Leninist victory.

In each of these conflicts one of the parties has pursued its goals by violence. Both traditionalist death squads and murderous guerrillas have attacked political party, labor and peasant leaders working to establish and consolidate democratic institutions, killing them and dismantling their efforts to build democracy.

The co-existence of these conflicts greatly complicates the task of the democratic forces and their friends. Each violent group attempts to hide behind the other. Neither group has been willing to subordinate its desire for power to the civilized disciplines of the democratic process. The violence of the death squads weakens fragile democratic institutions at a time when they are already under attack by communist guerrillas. It wipes out democratic leaders, intimidates the less hardy, undermines freedom, and hampers the forces of democracy in their struggle against the armed guerrillas. Marxist-Leninist violence imposes the economic and social strains of war on El Salvador at the same time that it kills Salvadorans, progressively destroys the economy, disrupts and intimidates the democratic leaders and others, and weakens those struggling to consolidate democratic institutions.

Both violent groups are morally and politically repugnant to this Commission, which strongly supports the consolidation and defense of democratic institutions in El Salvador.

In previous chapters, the Commission has proposed a number of measures designed to encourage and assist Salvadorans in the consolidating of democratic institutions and strengthening the rule of law, including technical assistance for elections, economic and education programs. In this chapter we recommend "conditioning" military assistance to the government of El Salvador on progress in the effort to bring death squads under control.

It is not only for the sake of democratic reform and human rights that we oppose the death squads. Their violent attacks upon Salvadoran democrats handicap the struggle to resist the armed insurgency of the guerrillas. This Marxist insurgency not only opposes democracy and is committed to the violent seizure of power, but also threatens U.S. security interests because of its ties to Nicaragua, Cuba, and the Soviet Union. The policy challenge facing the United States is to untangle these two conflicts—to support the forces of democratic reform against the death squads while at the same time helping El Salvador resist subjugation by Marxist-Leninist guerrillas.

A major goal of U.S. policy in Central America should be to give democratic forces there the time and the opportunity to carry out the structural reforms essential for that country's security and well-being.

Because this chapter addresses the question of security, it will focus initially on the threat posed by Marxist-Leninist insurgencies in Central America. It will then put forward proposals to end human rights abuses by the death squads.

The externally supported guerrilla insurgency that confronts us in El Salvador and elsewhere in Central America is really a new kind of war. It differs as much from indigenous revolts as it does from conventional wars. It is more complex, both in concept and in execution. By now the world has had enough experience with it so that its nature is known and its patterns are predictable.

An examination of any particular externally supported insurgency requires an understanding of a) the internal conditions that invited it, and b) the external forces that support it. Both are essential elements, and the interaction between them is one of the key factors that make these wars so difficult for governments to win and so devastating for the people who become their victims.

The Path of Insurgency

Cuba and Nicaragua did not invent the grievances that made insurrection possible in El Salvador and elsewhere. Those grievances are real and acute. In other chapters we have discussed ways of remedying them. But it is important to bear in mind three facts about the kind of insurgencies we confront:

- They depend on external support, which is substantially more effective when it includes the provision of privileged sanctuaries for the insurgents.
- They develop their own momentum, independent of the conditions on which they feed.
- The insurgents, if they win, will create a totalitarian regime in the image of their sponsors' ideology and their own.

Let us first take these three points, briefly, in order, and then examine them more fully in the particular context of the struggle now going on in Central America.

EXTERNAL INTERVENTION. Whatever the social and economic conditions that invited insurgency in the region, outside intervention is what gives the conflict its present character. Of course, uprisings occur without outside support, but protracted guerrilla insurgencies require external assistance. Indeed, if wretched conditions were themselves enough to create such insurgencies, we would see them in many more countries of the world.

Propaganda support, money, sanctuary, arms, supplies, training, communications, intelligence, logistics, all are important in both morale and operational terms. Without such support from Cuba, Nicaragua and the Soviet Union, neither in El Salvador nor elsewhere in Central America would such an insurgency pose so severe a threat to the government. With such support, guerrilla forces could develop insurgencies in many other countries. The struggle in El Salvador is particularly severe because it is there that external support is at present most heavily concentrated.

Therefore, curbing the insurgents' violence in El Salvador requires, in part, cutting them off from their sources of foreign support.

INDEPENDENT MOMENTUM. If reforms had been undertaken earlier, there would almost surely have been no fertile ground for revolution, and thus no effectively developed insurgency. But once an insurgency is fully under way, and once the lines of external support are in place, it has a momentum which reforms alone cannot stop. Unchecked, the insurgents can destroy faster than the reformers can build.

One reason for this is that an explicit purpose of guerrilla violence is to make matters worse: to paralyze the economy, to heighten social discords, to spread fear and despair, to weaken institutions and to undermine government authority—all so as to radicalize the people, and to persuade them that any alternative is better than what they have. By disrupting order, the strategy of terror strikes at the foundation of authority. By helping to provoke the use of counter-terror, as Carlos Marighella wrote in his classic terrorist tract, *Minimanual of the Urban Guerrilla*, guerrillas can transform "the political situation in the country . . . into a military situation in which the militarists appear more and more to be the ones responsible for terror and violence, while the problems in the lives of the people become truly catastrophic."

None of this legitimizes the use of arbitrary violence by the right in El Salvador or elsewhere. Indeed, the grim reality is that many of the excesses we have condemned would be present even if there were no guerrilla war supported by outside forces. But this analysis does explain why political, economic and social programs do not by themselves defeat these insurgencies, though they address a central part of the problem. If the reforms are to be effective, the violence must be checked—which means that the security situation must be improved dramatically.

THE TOTALITARIAN OUTCOME. Because the Marxist-Leninist insurgents appeal to often legitimate grievances, a popular school of thought holds that guerrilla leaders are the engines of reform. They characteristically reinforce this by inviting well-meaning democratic leaders to participate in a Popular Front, taking care, however, to retain in their own hands a monopoly of the instruments of force. If the insurgents were in fact the vehicles for democratic and social progress, the entire security issue would be moot; they would no longer be the problem, but rather the solution.

Unfortunately, history offers no basis for such optimism. No Marxist-Leninist "popular front" insurgency has ever turned democratic *after* its victory. Cuba and Nicaragua are striking examples. Regimes created by the victory of Marxist-Leninist guerrillas become totalitarian. That is their purpose, their nature, their doctrine, and their record.

The Cuban-Soviet Connection

In retrospect it is clear that Castro's communization of Cuba was a seminal event in the history of the Americas—a fact appreciated almost immediately by the Soviet Union. It prompted Khrushchev to declare in 1960 that the Monroe Doctrine had "outlived its times" and had died "a natural death."

Soviet policy in this hemisphere has followed the pattern of Soviet policy elsewhere in the world: Moscow has exploited opportunities for the expansion of Soviet influence. In the aftermath of the Cuban Missile Crisis, the Soviets concentrated on expanding their diplomatic, economic and cultural ties in Latin America and on strengthening the influence of local communist parties in broad electoral fronts, trade unions and the universities. In this respect they differed from Castro, who continued to support a course of armed struggle in Venezuela, Colombia, Guatemala, and several other countries. But later the fall of Allende in Chile and the subsequent right-wing takeovers in Uruguay, Argentina, and Bolivia discredited the Soviet expectation of the "peaceful path" to communism in Latin America.

In the 1970's, a number of other developments combined to shift the Soviet Union toward a more adventurous approach, including support for revolutionary armed struggle in Central America.

One of these developments was the triumph of Soviet-backed forces in Indochina, Angola, Mozambique, Ethiopia and South Yemen. This seemed to reward a more aggressive Soviet policy toward the Third World generally, in keeping with the perception in Moscow that the "correlation of forces" had shifted dramatically against the West.

The result was a very significant strengthening of the Soviet military capability in the Caribbean. This included a dramatic build-up in the size and sophistication of the Cuban Armed Forces, not least their air and naval components; an enlarged direct Soviet military presence in Cuba, with regular port calls by Soviet naval task forces and nuclear missile submarines and the deployment of advanced reconnaissance aircraft; increased numbers of Soviet military advisers; and close operational collaboration between Soviet and Cuban forces, as, for example, when Russian pilots were sent to Cuba in 1976 and 1978 to replace Cuban pilots aiding pro-Soviet regimes in Angola and Ethiopia.

This coincided with a reduction in the U.S. military presence in the Caribbean Basin (from over 25,000 in 1968 to under 16,000 in 1981), in the wake of Vietnam and in a climate of public hostility to U.S. security concerns, especially in the Third World.

Finally, the 1970's saw the sharpening of the social, economic, and political crisis in Central America—a development extensively dealt with elsewhere in this report—which made the region an inviting target for insurgency.

The success of the revolution in Nicaragua in 1979, like Castro's own accession to power a decisive event, accelerated the revision of Soviet policy toward revolution in Central America.

The President of the Soviet Association of Friendship with Latin American countries, Viktor Volski, called the armed victory in Nicaragua a "model" to be followed in other countries, while Boris Ponomarev, the chairman of the International Department of the Central Committee of the Soviet Communist Party, included the countries of Central America for the first time among Third World states undergoing revolutionary changes of "a socialist orientation."

Cuban and Soviet perceptions began to merge again. The new line was quickly accepted by the Communist Party of El Salvador (PCES), which had previously described the country's insurgent groups as "adventurist" and "bound to fail," and had been accused, in turn, of "decadence" and "revisionism." The PCES now made a complete about-face and turned toward armed struggle. The Party Secretary General, Shafik Jorge Handal, wrote in *Kommunist*, the theoretical organ of the Soviet Communist Party, that the Salvadoran revolution "will be victorious by the armed road . . . there is no other way."

The revolutionary strategy pursued in 1978–79 by Cuba in Nicaragua has since been attempted in El Salvador, Guatemala, and Honduras. Traditionally splintered insurgent groups were required to unify as a condition for increased Cuban and other Soviet bloc military support. This creation of a unified military front allowed Cuba to exercise greater control over the uprising. Meanwhile, a separate political front was created—a "broad coalition," led by the extreme left but including some elements of the noncommunist opposition. Such a political front allowed the guerrillas to co-opt some noncommunist leaders and to neutralize them as rival alternatives to the existing government. This objective was also served by the insurgency itself, which undermined the political center by sharpening the increasingly violent confrontation between left and right. The popular-front tactic helped the guerrillas to disarm critics by posing as noncommunist democrats, to obtain noncommunist international support, and to attempt to isolate the targeted government from Western political and material help.

Cuba was in a position to back up this strategy with an institutional capacity to promote guerrilla warfare far greater than it had possessed during the 1960's. The principal instrument was the Americas Department of the Cuban Communist Party, established in Havana in 1974 to centralize Cuba's operational control over covert revolutionary activities throughout the hemisphere and particularly in Central America. The Department's activities also included supervision of a network of guerrilla training camps and indoctrination schools inside Cuba.

The commitment to the promotion of armed struggle was further backed up by a dramatic increase in Soviet arms deliveries to Cuba. They grew from an average of 15,000 tons a year in the 1970's—roughly equal to current deliveries to Nicaragua—to 66,000 tons in 1981, and about the same amount in each of the following two years. Cuba's armed forces currently total 227,000, a fivefold increase over 1960, and this figure does not include paramilitary and reserve organizations of 780,000. Cuban forces are well equipped with sophisticated weaponry supplied by Moscow, have extensive combat experience on foreign soil, and are well trained. In addition, the Soviets provide a brigade of approximately 3,000 men stationed near Havana, as well as an additional presence of 2,500 military advisers and 8,000 civilian advisers.

The Cuban Air Force now has more than 200 combat jet aircraft, including three squadrons of Mig-23's, as well as Mi-8 helicopter gunships and Mi-24 assault helicopters. AN-26 and other transport aircraft give Cuba a logistic capability much greater than it had at the time of the airlift to Angola in 1975. An expansion of the Cuban Navy which began in the 1970's has continued with the acquisition of two Foxtrot submarines, a Koni-class frigate, minesweepers, and landing craft, and an upgrading of the naval base at Cienfuegos, which services nuclear submarines.

All this makes Cuba no less than the second military power in Latin America after Brazil, a country with twelve times Cuba's population. And some experts put Cuba ahead of even Brazil in terms of modern military capabilities. Cuba's island geography complicates its sponsorship of subversion. But Nicaragua suffers no such limitation. From there, men and materiel destined for El Salvador can be transported overland through remote areas by routes that are almost impossible to patrol on a constant basis, or by sea to isolated beaches, or by air at night to remote bush strips along the coast or farther inland. Furthermore, Cuba, with Soviet aid, has built a powerful radio communication center that is now being used to relay the orders of insurgent leaders based in Nicaragua to their troops in the field, thus making the Salvadoran guerrillas far more effective than would otherwise be possible.

As a mainland platform, therefore, Nicaragua is a crucial steppingstone for Cuban and Soviet efforts to promote armed insurgency in Central America. Its location explains why the Nicaraguan revolution of 1979, like the Cuban revolution 20 years earlier, was a decisive turning point in the affairs of the region. With the victory of the Sandinistas in Nicaragua, the levels of violence and counter-violence in Central America rapidly increased, engulfing the entire region.

Strategic Implications for the United States

Through most of its history, the United States has been able to take for granted our security in our own hemisphere. We have come to think, as Walter Lippmann wrote four decades ago, "that our privileged position was a natural right." In fact, it was the rivalries in Europe and the supremacy of British seapower that allowed us to uphold the Monroe Doctrine with minimal effort for more than a century—until the intrusion of communism into Cuba.

The ability of the United States to sustain a tolerable balance of power on the global scene at a manageable cost depends on the inherent security of its land borders. This advantage is of crucial importance. It offsets an otherwise serious liability: our distance from Europe, the Middle East, and East Asia, which are also of strategic concern to the United States. Security commitments in those areas require the United States to supply its forces overseas at the far end of transoceanic lines of communication whose protection can be almost as costly as the forces themselves.

At the level of global strategy, therefore, the advance of Soviet and Cuban power on the American mainland affects the global balance. To the extent that a further Marxist-Leninist advance in Central America leading to progressive deterioration and a further projection of Soviet and Cuban power in the region required us to defend against security threats near our borders, we would face a difficult choice between unpalatable alternatives. We would either have to assume a permanently increased defense burden, or see our capacity to defend distant troublespots reduced, and as a result have to reduce important commitments elsewhere in the world. From the standpoint of the Soviet Union, it would be a major strategic coup to impose on the United States the burden of defending our southern approaches, thereby stripping us of the compensating advantage that offsets the burden of our transoceanic lines of communication.

Such a deterioration in Central America would also greatly increase both the difficulty and the cost of protecting these lines of communications themselves. Under present plans, some 50 percent of the shipping tonnage that would be needed to reinforce the European front, and about 40 percent of that required by a major East Asian conflict, would have to pass from the Gulf of Mexico through the Caribbean-Central American zone. These same sea routes also carry nearly half of all other foreign cargo, including crude oil, shipped to this country.

The Soviets have already achieved a greater capability to interdict shipping than the Nazis had during World War II, when 50 percent of U.S. supplies to Europe and Africa were shipped from Gulf ports. German U-boats then sank 260 merchant ships in just six months, despite the fact that Allied forces enjoyed many advantages, including a two-to-one edge in submarines and the use of Cuba for resupply and basing operations. Today this is reversed. The Soviets now have a two-to-one edge overall in submarines and can operate and receive aircover from Cuba, a point from which all 13 Caribbean sea lanes passing through four chokepoints are vulnerable to interdiction.

The Soviet ability to carry out a strategy of "strategic denial" is further enhanced by the presence near Havana of the largest Soviet-managed electronic monitoring complex outside the Soviet Union, as well as by the regular deployment of TU-95 Bear naval reconnaissance aircraft.

Now there is the added threat of an entire new set of problems posed by Nicaragua. It already serves as a base of subversion, through overland infiltration of people and supplies, that can affect the entire region, Panama included. Panama is gradually assuming full responsibility for the security of the Canal; this means that any threat to the political security of that country and to the maintenance of its friendly relations with the United States automatically constitutes a strategic threat.

As Nicaragua is already doing, additional Marxist-Leninist regimes in Central America could be expected to expand their armed forces, bring in large numbers of Cuban and other Soviet bloc advisers, develop sophisticated agencies of internal repression and external subversion, and sharpen polarizations, both within individual countries and regionally. This would almost surely produce refugees, perhaps millions of them, many of whom would seek entry into the United States. Even setting aside the broader strategic considerations, the United States cannot isolate itself from the regional turmoil. The crisis is on our doorstep.

Beyond the issue of U.S. security interests in the Central American–Caribbean region, our credibility worldwide is engaged. The triumph of hostile forces in what the Soviets call the "strategic rear" of the United States would be read as a sign of U.S. impotence.

Thus, even in terms of the direct national security interests of the United States, this country has large stakes in the present conflict in Central America. They include preventing:

- A series of developments which might require us to devote large resources to defend the southern approaches to the United States, thus reducing our capacity to defend our interests elsewhere.
- A potentially serious threat to our shipping lanes through the Caribbean.
- A proliferation of Marxist-Leninist states that would increase violence, dislocation, and political repression in the region.
- The erosion of our power to influence events worldwide that would flow from the perception that we were unable to influence vital events close to home.

The Problems of Guerrilla War

Despite these high stakes, the debate over Central America has been polarized in the United States. One reason may be the seeming paradox in which important security questions are raised by small conflicts in an area which we have customarily neglected.

On the one hand, the territories involved are not large, and neither is the number of soldiers, policemen, and insurgents active in each country. The current amounts of U.S. military assistance are also not significant by global standards. In the last fiscal year, for example, U.S. military aid to all countries in Central America combined amounted to $121.3 million, or 3 percent of U.S. military assistance worldwide.

On the other hand, there is the extreme intricacy of the struggles. They proceed concurrently in the realms of internal politics, regional diplomacy, and the global East-West competition, including worldwide propaganda; they comprise both guerrilla and terrorist phenomena as well as more conventional confrontations among armed forces; and they are governed by very complicated interactions between violence in all its forms and the political, social, and economic circumstances of each country.

Thus what is being tested is not so much the ability of the United States to provide large resources but rather the realism of our political attitudes, the harmony of Congressional and Administration priorities, and the adaptability of the military and civil departments of the Executive. What is more, Central American realities often clash with our historical experience and with the disparity between our resources and those of the threatened countries.

The fundamental dilemma is as follows: both the national interests of the United States and a genuine concern for the long-term welfare of Central America create powerful incentives to provide all necessary assistance to defeat totalitarian guerrillas. At the same time one of the principal objectives of the guerrilla forces is to destroy the morale and efficiency of the government's administration and programs.

We thus labor under an immediate handicap. Unlike the Soviet Union in Afghanistan, the U.S. cannot—and should not—impose its own administration, even for such laudable objectives as implementing political, social and economic reforms; it cannot place its own experts in each village and town to gather political intelligence; and it cannot supervise the conduct of each soldier and policeman in all dealings with the population. For all these goals, the U.S. Government must rely on the abilities and good faith of the government under attack.

But that government—already fragile because of history and structure and conflicting attitudes—is being systematically weakened further by the conditions of guerrilla warfare in which it must function.

Much attention has been paid—correctly—to the shortcomings of the El Salvador government. But it is important—and only fair—to recall the many demands that have been made upon it and the progress that has been made in many fields. It carried out impressive elections in 1982, despite severe intimidations by the guerrillas, and will conduct another one this March. It has been going forward with an extensive land reform program. It allows debate, freedom of assembly, opposition and other aspects of democracy, however imperfect. Albeit belatedly and due to U.S. pressure, it is beginning to address the problem of right-wing violence. It has made offers to the insurgents to resolve the conflict through the political process. All of this has been done in the midst of a bitter war. It is a record that compares very favorably with El Salvador's past and with that of its neighbor, Nicaragua.

There is, of course, a darker side as well in El Salvador. The United States obviously cannot accept, let alone support, the brutal methods practiced by certain reactionary forces in Central America. Some of these actions are related to counter-insurgency. Their common denominator is the systematic use of mass reprisals and selective killing and torture to dissuade the civil population from participating in the insurgency or from providing any help for the insurgents. Historically, such reprisals, along with the static guard of key installations and the occasional ambush of betrayed insurgent bands, have often proved capable of preserving colonial rule and unpopular governments for a very long time, even centuries. Other violence has in fact nothing to do with insurgency at all. It is designed to terrorize opponents, fight democracy, protect entrenched interests, and restore reactionary regimes.

Whatever their aims, these methods are totally repugnant to the values of the United States. Much more enlightened counter-insurgency models were pursued in, for example, Venezuela and Colombia in the 1960's when military action was combined with positive economic and political measures. The methods of counter-insurgency developed over the last generation by the armed forces of the United States are consistent with such models. They depend upon gaining the confidence and support of the people and specifically exclude the use of violence against innocent civilians.

Yet these methods are expensive. In addition to continued action on the economic and social fronts, they require two forms of military action, to be carried out by two distinct types of forces. First, local popular militias must be formed throughout the country (with whatever minimal training is feasible and with only the simplest weapons) to prevent the insurgents from using terror to extract obedience. These must include members trained as paramedics to deliver basic health care, which evokes strong local support for these forces. Since this localized protective militia cannot be expected to resist any sustained guerrilla attack, U.S. counter-insurgency methods also require the availability of well-trained and well-equipped regular forces in adequate numbers. These methods assume that the regular units will be provided with efficient communications and suitable transport, notably helicopters, to enable them to provide prompt help for village militias under attack, and to allow them to pursue guerrilla bands on the move.

The present level of U.S. military assistance to El Salvador is far too low to enable the armed forces of El Salvador to use these modern methods of counter-insurgency effectively. At the same time, the tendency in some quarters of the Salvadoran military towards brutality magnifies Congressional and Executive pressures for further cuts in aid. A vicious cycle results in which violence and denial of human rights spawn reductions in aid, and reductions in aid make more difficult the pursuit of an enlightened counter-insurgency effort.

The combination of the tactical guidance given by U.S. advisers and levels of aid inadequate to support that advice creates a potentially disastrous disparity between U.S. military tactics and Salvadoran military resources. U.S. tactical doctrine abjures static defense and teaches constant patrolling. But this requires the provision of expensive equipment such as helicopters. In their absence, the Salvadoran military abandon their static defenses for intensive foot patrolling, only to find the strategic objective they had been guarding destroyed in their absence.

In the Commission's view it is imperative to settle on a level of aid related to the operational requirements of a humane anti-guerrilla strategy and to stick with it for the requisite period of time.

Another obstacle to the effective pursuit of anti-guerrilla strategy is a provision of current U.S. law under which no assistance can be provided to law enforcement agencies. This dates back to a previous period when it was believed that such aid was sometimes helping groups guilty of serious human rights abuses. The purpose of the legislation was to prevent the United States and its personnel from being associated with unacceptable practices. That concern is valid, but, however laudable its intentions, the blanket legal prohibition against the provision of training and aid to police organizations has the paradoxical effect, in certain cases, of inhibiting our efforts to improve human rights performance. For example, while it is now understood in the Salvadoran armed forces that human rights violations endanger the flow of U.S. assistance, in the police organizations there is no training to professionalize and humanize operations. And in Costa Rica, where the police alone provide that country's security, we are prevented from helping that democracy defend itself in even the most rudimentary fashion.

We therefore suggest that Congress examine this question thoroughly and consider whether Section 660 of the Foreign Assistance Act should be amended so as to permit—under carefully defined conditions—the allocation of funds to the training and support of law enforcement agencies in Central America.

A final problem is philosophical. Our historic tendency as a nation is to think about diplomacy and military operations as antithetical. The fact is that the principles outlined here will enhance the prospects of a political solution whose characteristics are outlined in the next chapter. Experience suggests that a lasting political solution will become possible only when the insurgents are convinced that they cannot win through force, and are therefore willing to settle for the next best option: taking advantage of opportunities for democratic competition and participation.

In this regard, a military stalemate will not enhance but rather would inhibit the prospects for a political solution, since it would confirm that the government cannot prevail. This is itself a chief goal of an insurgency that aims to undermine a government's legitimacy. In a guerrilla war, a stalemate is not the same as a balance of power. Moreover, while an insurgency can sustain itself over time if it has access to sanctuaries and external sources of support, there is nothing to suggest that a government, especially a weak one, can endure the cumulative toll of protracted conflict. A successful counter-insurgency effort is not a substitute for negotiations. But such an effort—the more rapid the better— is a necessary condition for a political solution.

The Situation in El Salvador

The war is at a stalemate—a condition that in the long term favors the guerrillas. They have relatively little popular support in El Salvador, but they can probably continue the war as long as they receive the sort of external support they are now getting.

The guerrilla front (the Farabundo Martí National Liberation Front—FMLN) has established a unified military command with headquarters near Managua. The dominant element of the five guerrilla groups making up the FMLN is now the People's Revolutionary Army (ERP), which is active in eastern El Salvador. ERP strategy is one of systematic attacks on the economic infrastructure, in order to precipitate an economic and political collapse, and military actions designed for political and psychological effect. The ERP leaders are keenly interested in the impact of guerrilla actions on international public opinion, especially in the U.S., where they hope to discourage further support for El Salvador's Government.

The number of guerrillas has remained basically unchanged for the last two years: there are an estimated 6,000 front-line guerrillas and a slightly larger number organized in militia and support units. But these latter forces have been increasingly well armed and involved in operations with the front-line forces. The insurgents can now put perhaps as many as 12,000 trained and armed fighters in the field. Currently the Salvadoran armed forces, including defense and public security forces, have about 37,500 men. That gives the government less than a 4-to-1 advantage over the insurgents. A ratio of 10 to 1 has generally been considered necessary for successful counter-insurgency, though this ratio varies by individual case and clearly depends upon the capability and mobility of the government forces. In any event, the guerrillas have been able to demonstrate an increasing ability to maneuver and to concentrate their forces, and to react to Salvadoran Army moves.

In 1983, as in the past, the war was characterized by a cyclical pattern, in which the initiative swung between government and guerrilla forces. The ebb and flow of field operations has enabled the guerrillas to strengthen their presence in the eastern departments over the past two years. In the absence of significant Salvadoran military forces, armed guerrillas operate at will throughout the countryside. They have established the rudiments of a civil administration and have enforced a tax regime in areas under their control. Increasingly, they are able to mass their forces and overwhelm isolated garrisons or ambush relief columns.

The severity of guerrilla attacks on the transportation and electrical network in the eastern departments has resulted in the effective isolation of much of that area. The nature and extent of guerrilla operations have led to speculation that the military objective of the guerrillas in the eastern departments might be the establishment of a ''liberated'' zone, as a prelude to the extension of the war into the central departments.

The situation is not uniformly favorable to the guerrillas. Their bases in San Vicente have been disrupted. They have lost their infrastructure in western El Salvador and have been unable to reconstitute their support network in the cities. But although the military situation continues to be essentially a stalemate, the guerrillas' campaign of economic disruption and sabotage has helped to devastate the Salvadoran economy. In large part due to the violence, the country's gross domestic product has declined 25 percent in real terms in the last four years. In eastern El Salvador, the economic decline has been even more precipitous.

In part, the Salvadoran military's difficulties in containing the guerrilla threat are related to manpower problems—their training, their retention, their equipment, and their development. About three quarters of the Salvadoran armed forces are deployed in static positions that protect fixed installations. This leaves insufficient maneuver forces to carry the war consistently to the guerrillas.

The Commission has heard testimony that as the end of the U.S. fiscal year approaches the Salvadoran armed forces husband ammunition and equipment until the scale of congressional appropriations for U.S. assistance becomes clearer. At present assistance levels there are critical shortages of basic equipment, including communications, medical equipment and airlift assets.

The Salvadoran armed forces have also suffered from inadequate command and control, coordination and leadership. A recent major reorganization of the military command structure is designed to achieve needed improvements in command and control and coordination, and to lead to a more aggressive prosecution of the war. But to end the stalemate will require much more in equipment and trained manpower.

The Insurgency in Guatemala

The insurgency in Guatemala is at a much lower level. There are about 2,500 guerrillas in four groups loosely organized under an umbrella organization. The guerrillas lost critical ground in the fall of 1982 and have not yet recovered. The guerrillas engage in harassment and terrorism but make no attempt to hold ground or to engage military units in sustained combat.

The Guatemalan Army continues to apply counter-insurgency tactics developed through 20 years of experience in the field. At the heart of these tactics is aggressive and persistent small-unit patrolling in areas of guerrilla activity. A key feature of the counter-insurgency effort has been the organization of about 400,000 *campesinos* and Indians into Civil Defense Forces. These forces are poorly armed—only about one in ten men in some units is armed with a gun, usually an M-1 rifle—but they provide security for villagers, go on patrol regularly and have taken heavy casualties in contacts with insurgents.

The positive aspect of the counter-insurgency program is civic action, in which the Guatemalan Army has a long tradition. Under Ríos Montt the armed forces provided food and housing materials to villages participating in the Civil Defense program. The Guatemalan government's financial crisis, however, has led to a slowdown of the civic action efforts.

The Guatemalan armed forces have been able so far to contain the insurgency without assistance from abroad. This relative success is due to a number of factors: long experience in counter-insurgency; the greater geographical difficulty the guerrillas have in obtaining supplies from Nicaragua, as contrasted with the Salvadoran case; and the more favorable conditions for counter-insurgency operations prevailing in the less densely populated backlands of Guatemala. But financial restrictions on the Guatemalan government and shortages of military supplies and spare parts could soon begin to limit the effectiveness of the Guatemalan counter-insurgency effort.

An even more serious obstacle in terms of the ultimate containment of armed revolt in Guatemala is the brutal behavior of the security forces. In the cities they have murdered those even suspected of dissent. In the countryside, they have at times killed indiscriminately to repress any sign of support for the guerrillas. Such actions are morally unacceptable. They are also self-defeating—as long as they persist, the conditions in which insurgency can appear and reappear will continue.

Other Regional Security Problems

Security problems of a different order exist elsewhere in the region. Cuban and Nicaraguan efforts to foment insurgency in Honduras have so far failed. But on its visit to Tegucigalpa, the Commission found a deep anxiety over the extraordinary military buildup in Nicaragua. The Sandinista armed forces far outnumber and out-gun those of Nicaragua's northern neighbor. The advantage of the aging Honduran air force would quickly disappear if the Sandinistas acquired a few high-performance aircraft. Although it is questionable whether Nicaragua as yet has the logistical and other capabilities needed to mount a conventional cross-border attack, the build-up points in the direction of their acquiring such capabilities. In the absence of a regional political settlement, Honduras will feel compelled to strengthen and modernize its armed forces.

Although the government of Costa Rica has proclaimed a policy of strict military neutrality in the region's conflicts, we found in that country, too, a sense of foreboding over the Nicaraguan military build-up. Costa Rica has no armed force, only a small civil guard and a rural constabulary. These police forces must patrol a dangerous border and guard a democracy threatened by Central America's turbulent political currents. The provisions of U.S. law under which no aid can be provided to police organizations create a particularly absurd situation for Costa Rica. Because of these provisions, we are unable to furnish badly needed assistance to forces dedicated to the safeguarding of democracy.

MILITARY ASSISTANCE

While important U.S. interests are engaged in El Salvador, and while we pay a high political price at home and abroad for assisting the armed forces there, the United States has not provided enough military aid to support the methods of counter-insurgency we have urged. At the same time, the United States cannot countenance the brutal alternative methods of counter-insurgency which wreak intolerable violence upon the civilian population. In our judgment, the current levels of military aid are not sufficient to preserve even the existing military stalemate over a period of time. Given the increasing damage—both physical and political—being inflicted on the economy and government of El Salvador by the guerrillas, who are maintaining their strength, a collapse is not inconceivable.

The Salvadoran Government's National Campaign Plan combines military operations with follow-up civic actions to restore agriculture and commerce. The plan is designed to provide secure areas within which the Salvadoran *campesino* can grow, harvest and market his crops, and where industry can again operate. The plan assumes that sufficient security can be established countrywide to reduce the insurgency at least to a low level within two years. But the government's forces must be significantly and quickly strengthened if the plan is to succeed. Their requirements include:

• Increased air and ground mobility, to enable the government forces to reach and assist static positions under attack and, eventually, to seek out and engage the guerrillas.
• Increased training to upgrade the forces tactically and to generalize further the use of modern, humane, counter-insurgency methods, including civic action as such. This last includes not only road building and basic engineering projects, but especially the provision of basic health care by paramedics.
• Higher force levels, to enable the government forces both to protect important installations and to carry the war to the guerrillas; at present the choice is between allowing the destruction of vital infrastructures, or the indefinite prolongation of the war.
• Greater stocks of equipment and supplies to support a consistent war effort.
• Improved conditions for the troops in order to retain trained personnel, particularly by providing medical evacuation; at present, for the lack of evacuation helicopters, the fatality rate is very high.

There might be an argument for doing nothing to help the government of El Salvador. There might be an argument for doing a great deal more. There is, however, no logical argument for giving some aid but not enough. The worst possible policy for El Salvador is to provide just enough aid to keep the war going, but too little to wage it successfully.

As we have already made clear in this report, the Commission has concluded that present levels of U.S. military assistance are inadequate.

We are not in a position to judge the precise amounts and types of increased aid needed. We note that the U.S. Department of Defense estimates that it would take approximately $400 million in U.S. military assistance in 1984 and 1985 to break the military stalemate and allow the National Campaign Plan to be carried out. The Department believes that thereafter assistance levels could be brought down to considerably more modest levels.

The Commission recommends that the United States provide to El Salvador—subject to the conditions we specify later in this chapter—significantly increased levels of military aid as quickly as possible, so that the Salvadoran authorities can act on the assurance that needed aid will be forthcoming.

The training and improvement of the Salvadoran forces to the point where they can effectively wage counter-insurgency will take time. Indeed, given the complexity of the internal as well as external problems confronting El Salvador, the situation there will remain precarious, even with increased military assistance. Such assistance alone cannot assure the elements of national unity and of will that are necessary for success. But it is the Commission's judgment that without such aid the situation will surely deteriorate.

The Commission has not undertaken an equally detailed study of the defense requirements of Honduras. Based on the testimony we have had, it is our judgment that increased U.S. military assistance to Honduras is needed for training and equipment in order to build a credible deterrent and to meet renewed efforts at insurgency. The Administration should submit to the Congress an appropriate program in that regard.

Under suitable conditions, assistance to Guatemala to enable that country to pursue a more consistent and humane counter-insurgency strategy would be advisable. This question is treated below.

Other Measures

To be effective, U.S. military assistance programs require greater continuity and predictability. As we have seen, local commanders are now uncertain whether an adequate supply of such critical support items as ammunition will be on hand. The result in El Salvador has all too often been a less than vigorous prosecution of the war. *The Commission believes the Administration and the Congress should work together to achieve greater predictability. That could be most effectively achieved through multi-year funding.*

Additional issues the Commission believes require attention

but which we have not had the opportunity to examine in detail include:

- The length of the service tours of our military people in El Salvador.
- The development of greater area expertise by selected U.S. military personnel.
- Organization and command structure in the Pentagon and the field.
- Prospects for closer cooperation among the nations of Central America in defense matters.
- The possibility of a strengthened role for the Inter-American Defense Board.

We believe the National Security Council should conduct a detailed review of these issues.

HUMAN RIGHTS

The question of the relationship between military aid and human rights abuses is both extremely difficult and extremely important. It involves the potential clash of two basic U.S. objectives. On the one hand, we seek to promote justice and find it repugnant to support forces that violate—or tolerate violation of —fundamental U.S. values. On the other hand, we are engaged in El Salvador and Central America because we are serving fundamental U.S. interests that transcend any particular government.

Our approach must therefore embrace, and pursue, both objectives simultaneously. Clearly, sustained public and international support rests heavily on our success in harmonizing our dual goals. Against this background, we have stressed the need to make American development assistance strictly conditional on rapid progress towards democratic pluralism and respect for human rights, as well as economic performance. Respect for human rights is also of great importance to improved security in Central America, as well as to the self-respect of the United States. We recognize, however, that how the problem is addressed in this regard is vital because Central America is crucial to our national security.

While the objectives of security and human rights are sometimes counterposed against each other, they are actually closely related. Without adequate military aid, Salvadoran forces would not be able to carry out the modern counter-insurgency tactics that would help keep civilian losses to a minimum. Were military aid to be cut off, it would open the way for the triumph of the guerrillas, an eventuality that no one concerned about the well-being of the Salvadoran people can accept with equanimity. Such a development would be unacceptable from the standpoint of both human rights and security.

The Commission believes that vigorous, concurrent policies on both the military and human rights fronts are needed to break out of the demoralizing cycle of deterioration on the one hand and abuses on the other. We believe policies of increased aid and increased pressure to safeguard human rights would improve both security and justice. A slackening on one front would undermine our objective on the other. El Salvador must succeed on both or it will not succeed on either.

The United States Government has a right to demand certain minimum standards of respect for human rights as a condition for providing military aid to any country.

With respect to El Salvador, military aid should, through legislation requiring periodic reports, be made contingent upon demonstrated progress toward free elections; freedom of association; the establishment of the rule of law and an effective judicial system; and the termination of the activities of the so-called death squads, as well as vigorous action against those guilty of crimes and the prosecution to the extent possible of past offenders. These conditions should be seriously enforced.

Implementation of this approach would be greatly facilitated through the device of an independent monitoring body, such as the Central American Development Organization spelled out in Chapter 4.

As an additional measure, the United States should impose sanctions, including the denial of visas, deportation, and the investigation of financial dealings, against foreign nationals in the United States who are connected with death-squad activities in El Salvador or anywhere else.

It is the Commission's judgment that the same policy approach should be employed in the case of Guatemala. The existing human rights situation there is unacceptable and the security situation could become critical. Although the insurgency in Guatemala has been contained for the time being at a relatively low level, military assistance could become necessary. Military aid and military sales should be authorized if Guatemala meets the human rights conditions described in this chapter. In terms of regional and U.S. security interests, Guatemala, with its strategic position on the Mexican border, the largest population in the Central American area and the most important economy, is obviously a pivotal country.

Conclusion

The Commission has concluded that the security interests of the United States are importantly engaged in Central America; that these interests require a significantly larger program of military assistance, as well as greatly expanded support for economic growth and social reform; that there must be an end to the massive violation of human rights if security is to be achieved in Central America; and that external support for the insurgency must be neutralized for the same purpose—a problem we treat in the next chapter.

The deterioration in Central America has been such that we cannot afford paralysis in defending our national interests and in achieving our national purposes. The fact that such paralysis resulted from the lack of a national consensus on foreign policy in the United States would not mitigate the consequences of failure. We believe that a consensus is possible, and must be achieved, on an issue of such importance to the national security of the United States.

We would hope, moreover, that a clear U.S. commitment to such a course would itself improve the prospects for successful negotiations—so that arms would support diplomacy rather than supplant it.

CHAPTER 7

THE SEARCH FOR PEACE

AMERICANS yearn for an end to the bloodshed in Central America. On no issue in the region is there a stronger consensus than on the hope for a diplomatic solution that will stop the killing and nourish freedom and progress. The Commission shares this deeply felt goal.

Yet simply to endorse a wish for peace is futile. Our duty is to try to define the means to achieve it.

U.S. diplomacy toward Central America can be neither conducted nor considered in a vacuum. It must reflect the larger realities of the hemisphere and of the world. It must also clearly embody a sustainable strategy for promoting U.S. interests in the region for the long-term. That strategy will involve many factors. What precise measures should be adopted, what trade-offs made, what balances struck, what responsibilities assumed by us and by others are proper subjects for debate. But we must be clear on:

- The context of our diplomacy.
- The nature of our objectives.
- The constancy of our policy.

History and experience both teach that effective diplomacy requires the coordination of many elements. Incentives for progress are essential. So are penalties for failure. Often, friendly forces need to be bolstered by both economic and security assistance. Aggressors must be made aware that unacceptable behavior carries risks. They must also know that a different pattern of behavior can bring significant benefits.

A successful political strategy in Central America must have certain basic underpinnings. It requires:

- Significant resources to promote economic progress.
- Vigorous efforts to advance democracy and social reform.
- Other inducements and penalties, short of force, to reinforce our diplomacy.

At the same time, there is little doubt that the projection of U.S. power, in some form, will be required to preserve the interests of the United States and of other nations in the region. A nation can project power without employing its forces in military encounter. However, a basic rule of statecraft is that assessment of risks is the solvent of diplomacy. In this case, we can expect negotiations to succeed only if those we seek to persuade have a clear understanding that there are circumstances in which the use of force, by the United States or by others, could become necessary as a last resort.

Successful diplomacy must also look beyond tomorrow's headline, next month's military setback, or next season's array of political contests. It must be based on support that can be maintained politically in the United States, as well as in other countries whose aid might be essential. Designing a set of policies which can command bipartisan backing in the United States is thus an essential foundation for diplomatic strategy. Without such support, we risk being mired in uncertainty, and caught up constantly in emergency assessments of what is politically possible in the United States rather than what is diplomatically attainable in Central America. In addition, unless U.S. strategy takes full account of the views, interests, and capacities of other affected nations in the area, we will not be able to forge the cooperation based on mutual respect which is the essence of the new approach we will outline here.

The general strategic objective that should animate U.S. diplomacy in dealing with the present threats in Central America can be simply stated: to reduce the civil wars, national conflicts and military preparations there at least to the dimensions of the Central American region.

As a nation we are certainly not opposed to indigenous reform in Central America. In Chapter 4 the Commission has put forward a program to encourage such reforms. Nor are we threatened by indigenous revolutions that use local resources and appeal to local circumstances.

What gives the current situation its special urgency is the external threat posed by the Sandinista regime in Nicaragua which is supported by massive Cuban military strength, backed by Soviet and other East bloc weapons, guidance and diplomacy, and integrated into the Cuban network of intelligence and subversion.

In considering the requirements for successful diplomacy in the region we should learn from our experience since 1962. The euphoria surrounding the resolution of the Cuban missile crisis in that year seemed to open the prospect that the Cuban revolution would at least be confined to its home territory. As President Kennedy put it in his news conference of November 20, 1962, ". . . if all offensive weapons systems are removed from Cuba and kept out of the hemisphere in the future, and if Cuba is not used for the export of aggressive communist purposes, there will be peace in the Caribbean."

This was more than an expectation. It was a declared policy objective of the United States. Obviously, it has not been achieved. The problem has been that it was eroded incrementally. This often made it difficult to see the erosion clearly, and, as a practical matter, made it even more difficult to halt at any given point. The increases in the Cuban threat were always so gradual that to stop them would have required making a major issue of what was, at the time, only a small change. The total effect of such small changes, however, has been—over five Administrations of both political parties—an enormously increased military power and capacity for aggression concentrated on the island of Cuba, and the projection of that threat into Central America (as well as into Africa and the Middle East).

This is not to assess blame. It is to sound a note of caution. Mutual restraint, settlement and peace are among the highest aspirations of mankind. But progress toward such goals can be difficult to measure. Words like "offensive weapons" and "aggression" are slippery. They can be made to mean different things in differing circumstances. And negotiators cannot anticipate the exact circumstances of the future.

Any agreement in Central America must be verifiable.

Equally important, it should also avoid any possible loophole that would permit the Soviet Union and Cuba to argue that whatever is not specifically prohibited is allowed. We should make sure that any agreement we reach is unambiguous. We should also remember that language and legalisms alone, however well crafted, will not provide airtight assurances in future cases not foreseen in the drafting. It will be important to give clear expression to the spirit of whatever obligations are undertaken, and to monitor continually how that spirit is respected. We must guard carefully against a gradual erosion of our position in any agreement worked out in Central America.

Finally, we need constancy in the pursuit of our goals. If we keep altering course with every shift in the wind, our adversaries will have no incentive to negotiate seriously. Doing so invites them to procrastinate; it also invites continual pressure on us to improve our offers. If, however, they find themselves confronted by a steady, persistent United States, holding firmly to a position that is reasonable, coherent and consistent, they will be more likely to calculate that time is not on their side. They will therefore be more prepared to make concessions that produce a reasonable agreement.

In sum, we believe that there is a chance for a political solution in Central America if the diplomacy of the United States is strategic in conception, purposeful in approach, and steadfast in execution. Our broad objectives should be:

- To stop the war and the killing in El Salvador.
- To create conditions under which Nicaragua can take its place as a peaceful and democratic member of the Central American community.
- To open the way to democratic development throughout the isthmus.

El Salvador

Obviously, the future of Central America will depend in large part on what happens in El Salvador. That nation most immediately faces critical choices about the course of its internal politics; it is wracked more severely by internal strife and conflict than any of its neighbors; it most requires intelligence and subtlety in the day-to-day conduct of U.S. diplomacy.

The dilemma in El Salvador is clear. With all its shortcomings, the existing government has conducted free elections. But it is weak. The judiciary is ineffective. The military is divided in its concerns, and in the degree of its respect for human rights. Privileged Salvadorans want to preserve both their political and economic power.

We have described in other chapters the economic, social and security measures we believe are necessary to make progress in economic development.

In the political field two broad options have been presented: either elections, or what is commonly referred to as power-sharing.

The government of El Salvador has consistently stated that a solution to the conflict "must be essentially political and democratic." This means that a political solution must result from the free choice of the Salvadoran people expressed through elections. The political parties represented in the Constituent Assembly, from the center-left Christian Democrats to the right-wing ARENA party, have formally endorsed this view. The United States has supported this position.

The Salvadoran Peace Commission was established last year —again in consultation with the political parties—for the "purpose of promoting the incorporation of all social and political sectors in the democratic process." The Commission has offered to discuss with the guerrilla fronts, the FMLN/FDR, the conditions under which the left could take part in the elections scheduled for March 25, 1984. The issues of security guarantees, access to the media and freedom to campaign would be included in such discussions.

The insurgents have rejected this offer. They assert that their security could not be assured. In any event, they hope for a collapse of American support, and eventually for a military victory. They evidently want to maintain unity among the various guerrilla groups, which they perceive would be put at risk by rifts over tough political decisions. They may well judge that a contested election would reveal their low level of popular support. So they seem to have cast their lot with continued military struggle unless the government is prepared to abandon the scheduled elections and install a coalition government.

The insurgents most recently set forth their formal position in September of last year, following contacts with Ambassador Richard Stone and the Salvadoran Peace Commission. In a document entitled "The Situation of Human Rights in El Salvador in Light of the Geneva Convention" and under the heading "Prospects for a Political Solution," the Political-Diplomatic Commission of the FMLN/FDR stated: "the Salvadoran people need a negotiated settlement between the government and the FMLN/FDR—to bring about peace; they do not need elections." The document went on to detail the FMLN/FDR position calling for comprehensive negotiations on the following agenda:

a) Composition of a provisional government.
b) Restructuring the armed forces.
c) Structural reforms.
d) Salvadoran foreign policy.
e) Mechanisms for future elections.
f) The process to achieve a ceasefire.

This is more than a refusal to campaign under the currently insecure conditions in El Salvador. Evidently the insurgents do not view power-sharing as merely an interim measure needed in order to hold elections in which the left could participate with security. Rather, it is a means of scrapping the existing elected governmental structure and armed forces and creating a provisional civil and military authority in their place in which the rebel leadership would have a major role—and in which they would eventually gain a dominant position well before the electoral "mechanisms" were in place.

Therefore, the Commission has concluded that power-sharing as proposed by the insurgents is not a sensible or fair political solution for El Salvador. There is no historical precedent suggesting that such a procedure would reconcile contending parties which entertain such deeply held beliefs and political goals, and which have been killing each other for years. Indeed, precedent argues that it would be only a prelude to a take-over by the insurgent forces.

To install a mixed provisional government by fiat would

scarcely be consistent with the notion that the popular will is the foundation of true government. It would tend to inflate the true strength of insurgent factions that have gained attention thus far through violence and their ability to disrupt the functioning of government. It would provide openings for them and their foreign supporters to forestall democratic politics. The likely final outcome of power-sharing would be the imposition on the people of El Salvador of a government unwilling to base its authority on the consent of the governed.

We believe that a true political solution in El Salvador can be reached only through free elections in which all significant groups have a right to participate. To be sure, elections do not solve a nation's problems. They can be the beginning, but cannot be the end, of political development. This is particularly true in El Salvador, which is threatened by a fragmentation of political life affecting most, if not all, of its institutions.

How elections are conducted will be crucial. Given prevailing conditions in El Salvador, all factions have legitimate concerns about their security. Neither supporters nor opponents of the regime can be expected to participate in elections so long as terrorists of the right or the left run free. No political efforts at reconciliation can succeed if the Government of El Salvador itself aids and abets violence against its own people. Unless it effectively curbs the actions of the death squads—unless it provides basic security for teachers, editors and writers, labor and religious leaders, and generally for the free and secure expression of opinion, the political process recommended here will break down. A secure environment must be established for all who wish to take part, whether leftists, centrists or rightists. The U.S. Government—to be credible—must insist that these conditions be met.

Thus the El Salvador Government must take all appropriate measures to make the March 25 elections as safe and open as possible. This should include the introduction of outside observers to help insure the security and fairness of the process.

The political process should not—indeed cannot—stop after the March elections. Following the elections, basic U.S. strategy for El Salvador should include firm support for the newly elected legitimate government. Along with providing military assistance, we should encourage it to pursue negotiations and reconciliation with all elements of Salvadoran society that are prepared to take part in an open and democratic political process, to promote rapid progress towards the protection of human rights, to strengthen civilian authority, and to undertake comprehensive reform of both political and military institutions. Such reform is essential to the creation of a stable, democratic government and for the reconciliation of disparate elements within Salvadoran society. U.S. economic assistance should be a key instrument in helping to secure these ends.

Even if the insurgents do not take part in the March elections, their participation in subsequent elections—at least participation by those prepared to accept the results of the balloting—should be encouraged. The Commission believes that a proposal along the following lines—which amplifies the government's approach —would constitute a genuinely fair chance for all to compete peacefully for political power in El Salvador. The basic principle would remain that of consulting the popular will, not imposing a government on the people through power-sharing. It would test the intentions of the insurgents.

We understand that El Salvador contemplates holding municipal and legislative assembly elections in 1985. The elements of the following approach could be applied to that process.

1. *The Salvadoran government would invite the FDR-FMLN to negotiate mutually acceptable procedures to establish a framework for future elections.* Although the details of the framework would have to be worked out by the parties to the talks themselves, the United States would energetically support their efforts and encourage other appropriate arrangements for elections in which all parties could participate as a first step toward a peaceful settlement of the conflict.

2. *As part of this framework a broadly representative Elections Commission would be established, including representatives of the FDR-FMLN.* The Salvadoran Government would thus be inviting participation by the political front of the guerrilla movement in the conduct of elections. The Commission would help ensure that all parties could compete openly and safely and that all citizens could receive political literature,

attend meetings and rallies, discuss partisan issues freely, and cast their ballots without fear or intimidation. The insurgent opposition should have a significant voice and vote both in the Elections Commission and in developing security arrangements for the campaign and election. But this should not become a subterfuge for the sharing of power with regard to the responsibilities of government, which we have rejected in this report.

3. *Violence should be ended by all parties so that mutually satisfactory arrangements can be developed among the government, pro-government parties, the different opposition groups and insurgent groups for the period of campaigning and elections.* To that end, certain developments are needed. The Salvadoran security forces and guerrillas should cease hostilities against one another. Guerrilla terror against military, government, and economic targets should end. Civilian and military violence of the right should also end.

4. *A system of international observation should be established to enhance the faith and confidence of all parties in the probity and equity of arrangements for elections.* This might include senior advisers to the Elections Commission drawn from the OAS, Contadora nations or third countries agreed upon by all parties to the conflict.

In sum, the United States should make a maximum effort to help El Salvador to create a self-sustaining society dedicated to open participation in its political process, to social justice, and to economic freedom, growth and development. An El Salvador that works toward these goals deserves our continuing support. This should include adequate levels of economic and military aid, which in turn can produce pressure for a politically negotiated end to the fighting.

What happens in El Salvador will have important consequences in the other nations of Central America. If the shaky center collapses and the country eventually is dominated by undemocratic extremes, this will lead to increased pressures on El Salvador's neighbors. For Guatemala and Nicaragua, the experience of El Salvador could carry a clear message: the best means of earning the support of the United States, and of promoting political, social, and economic development, lies in adopting both the form and the substance of democracy.

In addition, events in El Salvador will have a major impact on developments in Nicaragua and on Nicaragua's relations with its neighbors. It is to these factors that we now turn.

Nicaragua

The basic threat posed by Nicaragua has been examined in previous chapters. The Sandinista military forces are potentially larger than those of all the rest of Central America combined. The government in Managua volunteered to this Commission an intelligence briefing which left no reasonable doubt that Nicaragua is tied into the Cuban, and thereby the Soviet, intelligence network. The Commission encountered no leader in Central America, including democratic and unarmed Costa Rica, who did not express deep foreboding about the impact of a militarized, totalitarian Nicaragua on the peace and security of the region. Several expressed the view that should the Sandinista regime now be consolidated as a totalitarian state, their own freedom, and even their independence, would be jeopardized. In several countries, especially those with democratic traditions, we met leaders who expressed regret and outrage that the revolution against Somoza—which their own governments had supported— had been betrayed by the Sandinistas.

For all of these reasons, the consolidation of a Marxist-Leninist regime in Managua would be seen by its neighbors as constituting a permanent security threat. Because of its secretive nature, the existence of a political order on the Cuban model in Nicaragua would pose major difficulties in negotiating, implementing, and verifying any Sandinista commitment to refrain from supporting insurgency and subversion in other countries. In this sense, the development of an open political system in Nicaragua, with a free press and an active opposition, would provide an important security guarantee for the other countries of the region and would be a key element in any negotiated settlement.

Theoretically, the United States and its friends could abandon any hope of such a settlement and simply try to contain a Nicaragua which continued to receive military supplies on the present scale. In practical terms, however, such a course would present major difficulties. In the absence of a political settlement, there would be little incentive for the Sandinistas to act responsibly, even over a period of time, and much inducement to escalate their efforts to subvert Nicaragua's neighbors. To contain the export of revolution would require a level of vigilance and sustained effort that would be difficult for Nicaragua's neighbors and even for the United States. A fully militarized and equipped Nicaragua, with excellent intelligence and command and control organizations, would weigh heavily on the neighboring countries of the region. This threat would be particularly acute for democratic, unarmed Costa Rica. It would have especially serious implications for vital U.S. interests in the Panama Canal. We would then face the prospect, over time, of the collapse of the other countries of Central America, bringing with it the spectre of Marxist domination of the entire region and thus the danger of a larger war.

The notion that the United States should cope with a Marxist-Leninist Nicaragua, militarily allied to the Soviet Union and Cuba, through long-term containment assumes an analogy between conditions in post-war Europe and the present circumstances of Central America. The experience of the post-war period, however, shows that containment is effective as a long-term strategy only where U.S. military power serves to back up local forces of stable allies fully capable of coping with internal conflict and subversion from without. In such circumstances, the United States can help to assure the deterrence of overt military threats by contributing forces in place, or merely by strategic guarantees.

On the other hand, where internal insecurity is a chronic danger and where local governments are unable to deal with externally supported subversion, a strategy of containment has major disadvantages. It would risk the involvement of U.S. forces as surrogate policemen. Any significant deployment of U.S. forces in Central America would be very costly not just in a domestic political sense but in geo-strategic terms as well. The diversion of funds from the economic, social, medical, and educational development of the region into military containment would exacerbate poverty and encourage internal instability in each of the countries that became heavily militarized.

Furthermore, the dangers facing the other Central American countries might actually grow if each side perceived that the other was tempted to use its increased military power. And the creation of garrison states would almost certainly perpetuate the armies of the region as permanent political elites. The hopes of true democracy would not be enhanced.

Therefore, though the Commission believes that the Sandinista regime will pose a continuing threat to stability in the region, we do not advocate a policy of static containment.

Instead, we recommend, first, an effort to arrange a comprehensive regional settlement. This would elaborate and build upon the 21 objectives of the Contadora Group. Within the framework of basic principles, it would:

- Recognize linkage between democratization and security in the region.
- Relate the incentives of increased development aid and trade concessions to acceptance of mutual security guarantees.
- Engage the United States and other developed nations in the regional peace system.
- Establish an institutional mechanism in the region to implement that system.

The original peace initiatives of Nicaragua have given little cause for optimism that we could move toward these objectives. The latest of the Sandinistas' formal proposals were presented to the United States Government and to the United Nations in October 1983 as four draft treaties purportedly prepared "within the framework of the Contadora process." The treaties would bind the parties to refrain from sending arms from one country to another in the region, and otherwise to end intervention, "overt or covert," in the internal affairs of other nations of the region. Significantly, these Sandinista proposals would prohibit exercises and maneuvers of the type United States and Honduran forces have carried out, while deferring the question of foreign advisers for later discussion.

More recently, after the U.S. actions in Grenada, Managua has hinted at some accommodations in its external and internal policies. The Commission is not in a position to judge the sincerity and significance of these various signals. But clearly they would require extensive elaboration and more concrete expression before they could give solid grounds for hope.

The Commission believes, however, that whatever the prospects seem to be for productive negotiations, the United States must spare no effort to pursue the diplomatic route. Nicaragua's willingness to enter into a general agreement should be thoroughly tested through negotiations and actions. We must establish whether there is a political alternative to continuing confrontation in the region. Every avenue should be explored to see if the vague signals emanating from Managua in recent weeks can be translated into concrete progress. Our government must demonstrate to the people of the United States and the peoples of the region that the U.S. earnestly seeks a peaceful settlement.

It is beyond the scope of this Commission's responsibilities to prescribe tactics for the conduct of these negotiations. As a broad generality, we do not believe that it would be wise to dismantle existing incentives and pressures on the Managua regime except in conjunction with demonstrable progress on the negotiating front. With specific reference to the highly controversial question of whether the United States should provide support for the Nicaraguan insurgent forces opposed to the Sandinistas now in authority in Managua, the Commission recognized that an adequate examination of this issue would require treatment of sensitive information not appropriate to a public report. However, the majority of the members of the Commission, in their respective individual judgments, believe that the efforts of the Nicaraguan insurgents represent one of the incentives working in favor of a negotiated settlement and that the future role of the United States in those efforts must therefore be considered in the context of the negotiating process. The Commission has not, however, attempted to come to a collective judgment on whether, and how, the United States should provide support for these insurgent forces.

A Framework for Regional Security

The Commission believes that a comprehensive regional settlement could be based on the principles enumerated below. Such a settlement would not imply the liquidation of the Sandinista Government or the formal abandonment of its revolutionary ideals, but only that it submit itself to the legitimating test of free elections. It is therefore not beyond the realm of possibility that Nicaragua, and the other nations of the region, would in the end embrace it. The basic framework would be an agreement on Central American security negotiated among the Central American "five" (Costa Rica, El Salvador, Guatemala, Honduras and Nicaragua), containing these key elements:

- Respect for the sovereignty, independence, and integrity of all Central American countries.
- A broad and concrete commitment to democracy and human rights.
- A verifiable commitment by each nation not to attack its neighbors; nor to transfer arms overtly or covertly to any insurgents; nor to train the military personnel of a Central American country; nor to practice subversion, directly or indirectly, against its neighbors.
- A verifiable commitment by each country not to possess arms that exceeded certain sizes, types, and capabilities. The total permissible scale of military forces in each nation could be stipulated as not to exceed an agreed level substantially lower than now. No military forces, bases, or advisers of non–Central American countries would be permitted.
- United States respect for and cooperation with the agreement. This would include a readiness to support the Central American military and security arrangements, and a commitment to respect whatever domestic arrangements emerge from legitimating elections, as long as there is continuing adherence to the basic principles of pluralism at home and restraint abroad.
- Commitments by all countries to pluralism, to peaceful political activity, and to free elections in which all political parties

would have a right to participate free of threat or violence. Particularly, the pledges by Nicaragua of July 1979 to the OAS, and reaffirmed by the Contadora group, would be fulfilled. All insurgent groups would stop military activity.

- Permanent verification. The United States would be prepared to offer technical assistance to ensure effective verification. The Contadora countries could play a major role.
- The Central American nations that are parties to the agreement could invite other countries to be associated with it. They could also request that others in the hemisphere undertake mutual pledges of non-interference.
- Adherence to the agreement would be a condition for participating in the development program outlined in Chapters 4 and 5. The Central American Development Organization would, as suggested there, maintain a continuing audit and review of compliance with the commitments to nonintervention abroad and democratization at home.
- Foreign and other ministers of the Central American members, together with the United States, Mexico, Panama, Colombia, and Venezuela as observers, would meet regularly to review the arrangement and compliance with it. The council would develop procedures for conflict-resolution among member states.

A program along these lines would end any reason for Nicaragua to continue to depend on Cuba for its security. It would open the way for Nicaragua to participate in a vastly expanded, integrated development program. It would also bar an American military base in Honduras. The Nicaraguan insurgents would be able to participate in Nicaraguan elections. The insurgents in El Salvador would continue to be free to participate in elections there.

A settlement of this nature would bring peace and stability to Central America. It would insulate the region from great power rivalry. Dilution of its terms would carry risks. A failure of negotiations because not every term was fulfilled would carry other risks. These considerations will have to be weighed in the negotiating process itself, which is properly the responsibility of the U.S. Government, not of this Commission.

In any event, we recognize that to negotiate such an ambitious arrangement will take imagination, patience, and perseverance. We cannot expect a sudden solution to the security problems of Central America, just as we cannot expect democracy and pluralism to bloom overnight. But we can measure progress. We can expect long and arduous negotiations. But the stakes are too high, and the alternatives too bleak, to shy away from the most determined efforts to succeed.

These efforts will be critically dependent on inducements for agreement and compliance. It is partly for this reason that the Commission has proposed the major financial and commercial incentives set forth in Chapter 4. We conceive of these new programs in trade, aid, investment, employment, health and education as an integral element in the search for peace in the region. Such incentives have the added value of demonstrating to the peoples in the region the benefits of productive relations with the United States and the West in general.

At the same time, this diplomacy must carry with it penalties for failure to comply with any agreement reached. These would include at least the loss of shared economic benefits—such as a major drop in external aid flows and denial of access to special trade advantages.

Finally, as part of the backdrop to diplomacy, Nicaragua must be aware that force remains an ultimate recourse. The United States and the countries of the region retain this option. There are, of course, non-military measures available that we have not yet used—for example, economic restrictions and reduction of diplomatic contact. As for the military option, the precise circumstances in which it might be considered essential to U.S. security are beyond the Commission's mandate. But we do urge that direct U.S. military action—which would have major human and political costs—should be regarded only as a course of last resort and only where there are clear dangers to U.S. security.

If Managua proves responsive to serious negotiations, hopeful vistas open up for the beleaguered peoples of Central America, including those of Nicaragua. This is the course that we would strongly prefer. We do not seek confrontation. We prefer to resolve the conflicts in the region peacefully. We would like to get on with the formidable challenge of improving the lives of everyone in the region, including Nicaraguans.

The Contadora Group

The United States has a strong interest in encouraging the nations of Central America to assume greater responsibility for regional arrangements. Our involvement will be more acceptable if it reflects a regional consensus. When countries of the region take the lead, when we are not perceived as imposing regional goals, the prospects of a constructive evolution based on shared purposes will increase. Thus, a key objective for the United States should be to promote the development of an independent system of regional relations, backed up by commitments of U.S. economic resources, diplomatic support, and military assistance. In the final analysis, for any regional arrangement to be lasting it must be able to count on U.S. support. But for it to be supported it must elicit the cooperation and good will of our sister republics to the south.

Successful regional diplomacy within Central America must be based upon the interests of the Central American countries themselves. These interests will have to be reflected in broader regional arrangements that impose mutual obligations, create shared incentives to respect national rights, and provide both for verification of compliance and penalties for violation.

The four neighboring Contadora countries—Colombia, Mexico, Panama and Venezuela—have been active and creative in trying to develop a regional diplomacy that can meet the needs of Central America. Their role has been constructive in helping to define issues and to demonstrate the commitment of key Latin American nations to pursue stability and peaceful evolution within the region.

To be sure, the interests and attitudes of these four countries are not identical, nor do they always comport with our own. The Contadora nations do not have extensive experience in working together, and the Contadora process has not yet been tested in terms of crafting specific policies to provide for regional security. Thus the United States cannot use the Contadora process as a substitute for its own policies. Experience has shown that the process works most effectively when the United States acts purposefully. When our policy stagnates, the Contadora process languishes. When we are decisive, the Contadora process gathers momentum.

Within this framework, the United States should actively encourage the Contadora process. We should continue to consult genuinely and regularly with its members. We should continue to support its 21-point program while urging a more specific settlement. Given the size and complexity of the task, it is not surprising that progress is often gradual and on a general level. As already noted, the principles of the regional framework set forth in the previous section are fully consistent with the Contadora program. Indeed these principles seek to give greater concreteness to that program. And whatever the role of the Contadora group in the actual fashioning of settlements, it will certainly be central in their implementation and supervision.

The Contadora countries are engaged in a bold new experiment. They deserve the gratitude and encouragement of all the nations in the hemisphere.

Cuba and the Soviet Union

Both the role played by the Sandinista regime in Central America and the threats in neighboring countries gain added importance for the region and for the United States because of Cuba's active engagement. As we have seen, Cuba has long been committed to revolutionary violence as an essential part of its ideology; indeed, that commitment is reflected in its national constitution. In turn, Cuba is closely allied with the Soviet Union and other communist bloc states, gaining support from them and promoting their interests in the Caribbean Basin region.

Over the years, Cuban conduct in the region has taken on forms never foreseen at the time of the Cuban missile crisis of 1962. In his proclamation of October 23, 1962, President Kennedy declared that:

the United States is determined to prevent by whatever means may be necessary, including the use of arms, the Marxist-Leninist regime in Cuba from extending, by force or the threat of force, its aggressive or subversive activities to any part of this hemisphere, and to prevent in

[143]

Cuba the creation or use of an externally supported military capability endangering the security of the United States.

In this section of the proclamation, President Kennedy was in fact quoting a Joint Resolution of the Congress which had been passed only a few weeks before.

Clearly, these goals have not been achieved. Since then, Cuba —supplied, trained, and supported by its Soviet mentors—has grown into a power with major offensive capability, as outlined in the previous chapter. Propped up economically and militarily by the USSR, Cuba has been able to bankroll, train, advise, and participate in insurgent movements in Guatemala, Nicaragua, Honduras, El Salvador, Bolivia, Venezuela, and elsewhere in the hemisphere.

Thus President Kennedy's vision of 1962 has given way to a vastly different reality in 1984. In 1962 the United States hoped that, by the exercise of American will and the projection of American strength, Cuba would be neutralized as a threat to Central and South America. More than twenty years later the threat is still there—and in guises that are arguably more dangerous to the stability of the region than the IRBMs of the 1960's.

The United States has a clear interest in reducing Cuba's role as a surrogate for the Soviet Union in the hemisphere. Yet because of their mutual dependence—Cuba in gaining arms, economic aid, and diplomatic support; the Soviet Union in gaining greater access to the region—it is not likely that the United States will be able to separate Moscow from Havana under present circumstances. As in the past, Moscow may at times seek to limit particular acts of Cuban adventurism within the region when such acts impose excessive risks, conflict with other Soviet objectives, or offer little opportunity. But Moscow is unlikely to be either able or willing to require Cuba to abandon its revolutionary principles and activity.

Should Havana, for whatever reason, change its basic attitude and be prepared for genuine coexistence with the United States, we, in turn, should be prepared to negotiate seriously. Such coexistence would have to involve an end to Cuban support for insurgency in Central America and promotion of revolutions elsewhere in the world. We, in turn, should then be prepared to live with Cuba and lift existing restrictions.

In the meantime, the United States has a dual task: to create those economic conditions in Central America that thwart the export of revolutions and to make clear the risks of expanded violence. Social reform, economic advance and political stability in Central America will discourage Cuban adventurism in the region. But we must also bring home to Havana a due appreciation of the consequences of its actions.

As for the Soviet Union, it has been pursuing a strategy of progressively greater involvement in the Western Hemisphere, particularly in reaching beyond Cuba to Central America and the Caribbean. It has employed gradualism, ambiguity, and proxies. For Moscow, this strategy has entailed few risks, either military or political; except in the case of Cuba, it has been inexpensive; and it has held the potential for significant gains. Soviet objectives, beginning with Cuba in the early 1960's, have been to end unchallenged U.S. pre-eminence within the hemisphere and possibly to see other "Cubas" established, to divert U.S. attention and resources from other parts of the world that are of greater importance to Moscow, to complicate our relations with our West European allies, and to burnish the Soviet Union's image as a revolutionary state.

Preserving U.S. interests in Central America and the Caribbean against the Soviet challenge will be a significant concern for years to come. We reject the proposition that the establishment of a Soviet military base in Central America is the sole, or even the major, threat to U.S. interests. Unless current Cuban-Nicaraguan designs are checked, long before Moscow feels ready for such a move the turmoil in Central America will have reached a point of crisis that could not be contained in Central American dimensions. In designing a basic policy toward the region, we must make the Soviet Union understand the limits of its activity, especially before its practice hardens into precedent. Moscow must be forestalled from making gains that would give it major advantages either within the region or in wider aspects of East-West relations.

Excluding Soviet involvement in Central America altogether

—extending to trade, diplomatic relations, and the gaining of some influence in individual countries—is no doubt impossible. At the other extreme, clearly any Soviet involvement in the region that poses a strategic threat to the United States is unacceptable. The policy questions are, first, to decide at what point between these two extremes of Soviet involvement the balance point of U.S. interests lies; and second, to take those actions necessary to preserve those interests.

The United States cannot accept Soviet military engagement in Central America and the Caribbean beyond what we reluctantly tolerate in Cuba.

We will also need to define specific situations as precisely as possible and to make those definitions clear to Moscow. At the same time we must avoid the inference that Soviet actions we have not proscribed are thus acceptable to us. If we do challenge directly any particular Soviet military activity in the region, we must be prepared to prevail.

On the other hand, some Soviet involvement in Central America and the Caribbean is likely to fall into gray areas. Except where a Soviet position of dominance is either imposed or preserved through force of arms, Moscow depends for its opportunities on conditions both within the region and within individual countries. Where political, social and economic programs forestall violent revolution, Soviet ability to fish in troubled waters is severely limited. Where we can agree with countries in Latin America that Soviet actions pose a threat to hemispheric interests, we can share leadership in opposing those actions. Where countries of the region can agree on mutual security and the pooling of benefits, collective actions can reduce Soviet opportunities.

Against this backdrop, the Commission sees little promise in negotiating with the Soviet Union over Central America. The Soviets would almost certainly use negotiations to legitimize their presence in the region. They would welcome discussion about superpower spheres of influence, which would prompt Soviet assertions of primacy and the need for U.S. abstention on the Soviet periphery, in such places as Eastern Europe and Afghanistan. For the United States, however, such a concept of spheres of influence is unacceptable. Should the United States now accept that concept, the Soviet Union would reap substantial gains.

In sum, the United States cannot eliminate all Soviet political involvement and influence within Central America and the Caribbean. But we must curb Soviet military activity in the hemisphere. And we can reduce Soviet opportunities and increase the incentives for others to abstain from forging ties with Moscow that damage U.S. and regional interests.

Western Europe

In developing a basic strategy toward Central America, we also need to take into account the policies and interests of our West European allies. Spain has important historical, cultural and economic ties to the region. Other European countries have modest economic concerns in the region and only occasional residual involvements, such as the British military presence in Belize. But none of them has vital stakes in the Western Hemisphere.

Their fundamental interest derives from our own, and it is not inconsiderable. As was seen in the previous chapter, the ability of the United States to fulfill its commitments to the Western Alliance would be adversely affected by developments in Central America that threatened the security of the Caribbean sea lanes (through which Europe would be resupplied in the event of a crisis) or that required a redeployment of U.S. forces to protect interests in this hemisphere. The European security interest in Central America is thus significant, even if it is indirect.

Unfortunately, this interest is not always well appreciated in Europe. Some European governments and political organizations have taken actions inimical to U.S.—and indeed, to European—security, such as supporting the Sandinista government or the Salvadoran insurgents. At the same time, some European governments have shown understanding of the difficult problems facing the United States in Central America.

The differences between the United States and Europe over Central America have diverse causes. In part they derive from differing views concerning the management of East-West and North-South relations. In addition, some Europeans see domestic political advantage in distancing themselves from us on issues in this hemisphere. In some instances, there is also political solidarity with revolutionary forces in the region.

Recently, allied expressions concerning Central America have been muted. This is partly due to a growing, though still inadequate, awareness by our allies that this region is of great political and security concern to the United States and therefore to themselves as well. They also are beginning to see that while there are some advantages in disassociation from U.S. policy in Central America, there are also costs in public disagreement with us. Not least, their recent restraint is also due to the increasingly widespread awareness in Europe that the Sandinistas have betrayed their revolution and threaten their neighbors.

The United States obviously cannot grant our European allies a veto over our policy decisions on Central America. At the same time, it is important that we regularly discuss our policies with them, and also discuss with them the rationale and factual basis for such policies. We should seek their political and diplomatic support where this is possible, and their restraint where it is not. We should strongly discourage their aiding the Sandinista regime, until it fundamentally changes course. And we should encourage their economic involvement in the region to help promote political, economic and social reform, both bilaterally and through multilateral institutions.

The Broader Efforts

The prospects for security and progress in Central America will turn on the efforts both of the nations of the region and of the United States. For the longer term, the primary emphasis must be upon the progressive reform of societies, the strengthening of political processes, and the improvement of economic conditions. To embrace these goals and provide the needed resources will not by itself assure security and progress. But without these broader efforts, no diplomatic strategy can be successful or endure.

There are no easy answers for the United States in Central America. There will be no early end to our domestic debate about the best course to follow. We must, nevertheless, vigorously pursue diplomatic and political approaches—together with the other strands of our policy—to foster a regional framework for security, peace, development and democracy.

CHAPTER 8

CONCLUSION

WE HAVE CONCLUDED this exercise persuaded that Central America is both vital and vulnerable, and that whatever other crises may arise to claim the nation's attention the United States cannot afford to turn away from that threatened region. Central America's crisis is our crisis.

All too frequently, wars and threats of wars are what draw attention to one part of the world or another. So it has been in Central America. The military crisis there captured our attention, but in doing so it has also wakened us to many other needs of the region. However belatedly, it did "concentrate the mind."

In the case of this Commission, one effect of concentrating the mind has been to clarify the picture we had of the nations of Central America. It is a common failing to see other nations as caricatures rather than as portraits, exaggerating one or two characteristics and losing sight of the subtler nuances on which so much of human experience centers. As we have studied these nations, we have become sharply aware of how great a mistake it would be to view them in one-dimensional terms. An exceptionally complex interplay of forces has shaped their history and continues to define their identities and to affect their destinies.

We have developed a great sympathy for those in Central America who are struggling to control those forces, and to bring their countries successfully through this period of political and social transformation. As a region, Central America is in mid-passage from the predominantly authoritarian patterns of the past to what can, with determination, with help, with luck, and with peace, become the predominantly democratic pluralism of the future. That transformation has been troubled, seldom smooth, and sometimes violent. In Nicaragua, we have seen the tragedy of a revolution betrayed; the same forces that stamped out the beginnings of democracy in Nicaragua now threaten El Salvador. In El Salvador itself, those seeking to establish democratic institutions are beset by violence from the extremists on both sides. But the spirit of freedom is strong throughout the region, and the determination persists to strengthen it where it exists and to achieve it where it does not.

The use of Nicaragua as a base for Soviet and Cuban efforts to penetrate the rest of the Central American isthmus, with El Salvador the target of first opportunity, gives the conflict there a major strategic dimension. The direct involvement of aggressive external forces makes it a challenge to the system of hemispheric security, and, quite specifically, to the security interests of the United States. This is a challenge to which the United States must respond.

But beyond this, we are challenged to respond to the urgent human needs of the people of Central America. Central America is a region in crisis economically, socially and politically. Its nations are our neighbors, and they need our help. This is one of those instances in which the requirements of national interest and the commands of conscience coincide.

Through the years, there has been a sort of natural progression in this nation's ties with other parts of the world. At first they were almost exclusively with Europe. Then, without diminishing those ties with Europe, we expanded our trans-Pacific bonds. Now the crisis in Central America has served as a vivid reminder that we need to strengthen our ties to the south, as well as east and west.

Our response to the present crisis in Central America must not be a passing phenomenon. The United States was born of a vision, which has inspired the world for two centuries. That vision shines most brightly when it is shared. Just as we want freedom for ourselves, we want freedom for others. Just as we cherish our vision, we should encourage others to pursue their own. But in fact, what we want for ourselves is very largely what the people of Central America want for themselves. They do share the vision of the future that our ideals represent, and the time has come for us to help them not just to aspire to that vision, but to participate in it.

[151]

Our task now, as a nation, is to transform the crisis in Central America into an opportunity: to seize the impetus it provides, and to use this to help our neighbors not only to secure their freedom from aggression and violence, but also to set in place the policies, processes and institutions that will make them both prosperous and free. If, together, we succeed in this, then the sponsors of violence will have done the opposite of what they intended: they will have roused us not only to turn back the tide of totalitarianism but to bring a new birth of hope and of opportunity to the people of Central America.

Because this is our opportunity, in conscience it is also our responsibility.

NOTES BY INDIVIDUAL
COMMISSIONERS

(Where these notes are addressed to specific issues in the Commission report, brackets indicate the pages of the report on which that issue is discussed.)

HENRY G. CISNEROS

The Commission report is a major contribution to U.S. thinking about its relations with the nations and peoples of Central America. I am in support of the vast majority of recommendations in the Commission report. There are however several fundamental issues which in my opinion require the statement of an alternate view. The following notes are my views on the issues discussed in Chapter 7, *The Search for Peace.*

[pp. 111–112] Strong steps must be taken to convince FDR/FMLN moderates with backgrounds of peaceful political struggle to take part in discussions concerning participation in a security task force to arrange security provisions for all participants on election processes. Many elements of the FDR, especially Social and Christian Democrats, actively contended for political power in elections as legal parties during the 1970's and their UNO coalition (which included both parties) ran José Napoleón Duarte and Guillermo Ungo as the presidential-vice presidential ticket in 1972 and won. It is important to note that a military coup prevented Duarte from taking office, that electoral fraud denied another UNO coalition ticket its rightful presidential victory in 1977, and that representatives of major FDR components, including Mr. Ungo, took part in the October 1979 reform junta strongly supported by the United States. Violence should be ended by all parties so that mutually satisfactory arrangements can be developed among the government, pro-government parties, and opposition groups for periods of campaigning and elections. As part of such security arrangements the Salvadoran security forces and the guerrillas should agree to a complete cease-fire and cessation of hostilities. Such discussions on the details of security arrangements and election matters are intended to determine the extent to which meaningful dialogue on coalition approaches and structural reforms can proceed.

[pp. 115–116] Nicaragua in October announced initiatives that suggest some possibilities for movement on negotiations concerning key aspects of relations among the countries in the region. More recently, Managua has taken other actions which should be encouraged to further internal conciliation. The Sandinista regime should be encouraged to intensify dialogue with the hierarchy of the Nicaraguan Catholic Church, the private sector, and the opposition parties; expand its offer of amnesty for anti-Sandinista rebels; introduce details of legislation to permit the free functioning of political parties and the promise of elections in 1985; eliminate censorship of the press; fulfill its recent promises to the opposition newspaper *La Prensa* to acquire newsprint; and reduce the numbers of Cuban advisers and Salvadoran rebel elements from Nicaragua. I believe further accommodation by the Nicaraguan regime to its internal opposition and to its neighbors can be encouraged through vigorous diplomacy by the United States. The United States should raise the standing of efforts to engage in diplomacy with Nicaragua as the most immediately hopeful means toward peaceful resolution of differences.

The United States should suspend "covert" aid to the anti-Sandinista rebels. The period for aid suspension should be through the year 1985 so that the Sandinista government can demonstrate its capacity to move toward pluralism and to fulfill its promise to hold free and fair elections in 1985. Such a step is intended to be matched by significant movement on the part of the Nicaraguan government to change policies which have aroused apprehension among its regional neighbors and is intended to reduce the risk of war between Nicaragua and Honduras. Success in changing Nicaraguan policies on external advisers, aid to Salvadoran insurgents, and the level of their military build-up should diminish the need for large increases in U.S. military aid to Honduras and El Salvador.

WILLIAM P. CLEMENTS, JR.

[pp. 107–108] I became convinced from the Commission's examination of the 1962 Kennedy-Khrushchev exchanges that those exchanges did not produce a meeting of the minds. I also believe that our policies since then have too often placed undue reliance on those exchanges as though they were a comprehensive agreement governing all aspects of U.S.-Cuban relations. I am convinced that there was no understanding or agreement.

CARLOS F. DIAZ-ALEJANDRO

As the introduction to this report wisely indicates, no document crafted by twelve persons will be completely satisfactory to each of them. While proud to associate myself with our report, I must go beyond that introductory *caveat* and register two points of fundamental disagreement.

[pp. 115–116] I believe that the type of covert support given by the United States government to Nicaraguan insurgents on balance hurts the chances of reaching the goal of a truly democratic Nicaragua. The net effect of such support is more likely to strengthen the most extremist sectors of the Sandinista leadership, and to allow them to claim patriotic motivation for bringing Nicaragua into closer military alliance with Cuba and the USSR. U.S. support to some insurgents is used by Managua to brand all dissidents as pawns of a foreign power, eroding the legitimacy of dissidence within Nicaragua, especially among the nationalistic youth, while giving Managua a handy excuse for economic failures and further political repression. The possibility of accidental war along the Nicaraguan northern border is also increased by these covert operations. Thus, rather than creating pressures for negotiations, U.S. support to Nicaraguan insurgents has made successful negotiations less likely. Under present circumstances, U.S. support to Nicaraguan democrats, if requested, should be overt and channelled primarily via the newly created Democracy Endowment and similar mechanisms.

[p. 55] In another crucial area, the timidity of the report in recommending a further opening of the U.S. market to Central American exports sharply contrasts with statements about the strategic importance of that region to the U.S. I believe that, under foreseeable circumstances, the most effective single policy for advancing long-term U.S. strategic interests in Central America would be to offer complete and unimpeded access to the United States market to exports from Central American countries joining the Development Organizations proposed in the report. Even with generous adjustment assistance to displaced U.S. workers and entrepreneurs, which I would favor, this policy would remain more cost-effective, over the long run, than direct economic and military aid.

HENRY A. KISSINGER
NICHOLAS F. BRADY
JOHN SILBER

[p. 102] We strongly endorse the objectives of the conditionality clause. We are also convinced that the United States extends military assistance to El Salvador above all to serve vital American political and security interests. We hope that both goals can be served simultaneously. We wish to record our strong view that neither the Congress nor the Executive Branch interpret conditionality in a manner that leads to a Marxist-Leninist victory in El Salvador, thereby damaging vital American interests and risking a larger war.

ROBERT S. STRAUSS

This report of the National Bipartisan Commission on Central America reflects valuable work done over the past months. The report provides the basis for continuing national debate about the best course for U.S. policy towards Central America in the years ahead. Its basic thrust is sound: that fundamental U.S. interests are at stake in Central America; that we must continue to be deeply engaged; that we need to develop a basic strategy that includes diplomatic, economic, and military elements; and that, to be sustainable, any U.S. approach must first earn and then command broad bipartisan support.

I file this note not in dissent to the report but because in my view in many Central American countries the creation and/or preservation of pluralistic government depends as much or more on a basic restructuring of internal political and social institutions as on military assistance. My concern is that this report, while not saying otherwise, might incorrectly be interpreted to the contrary.

WILLIAM B. WALSH

[p. 102] I am proud to have been a member of this Commission. The report represents the objective and serious conclusions of twelve members of diverse social and political background, whose prime concern was to suggest solutions for the Central American problem in an atmosphere of peace.

It is my feeling that conditionality must apply equally to all nations in the region. The proper revulsion with the activities of the "death squads" in El Salvador may give the reader the impression in this document that more severe restrictions have been placed upon that nation in qualifying for increased assistance than upon any other.

It is appropriate to recall that El Salvador has had a democratic election participated in by 80 percent of its population. More significantly, a second election is scheduled to be held on March 25, which will doubtless have the same media attention and international supervision as did the last election. Trade unions are functioning and political parties are permitted freedom of association and assembly with highly diverse views and actually participating in the electoral process. Concrete steps in response to demands by the Reagan Administration have been taken to reduce the activity of the death squads and to discipline those responsible for this activity. Participation of the extreme left has been invited in both the activities of the electoral commission and the political process. The left has rejected this opportunity in part because of fear, but primarily because of their belief they cannot win and because of their dedication to a military victory. No group dedicated to a Leninist philosophy can realistically be expected to participate in an electoral process which they cannot control. History is replete with the evidence for such a conclusion.

The government of El Salvador has a way to go—but the process has begun. Such process should be acknowledged and encouraged. Pluralism in the electoral process, personal freedom, and individual dignity are equally important in all nations in the region. Progress towards these objectives applies to all equally as a precedent for assistance.